CONCILIUM

D1519226

CONCILIUM   2004/5

A DIFFERENT WORLD IS POSSIBLE

Edited by
Luiz Carlos Susin, Jon Sobrino and Felix Wilfred

SCM Press · London

Published by SCM Press, 9–17 St Albans Place, London N1 0NX

Copyright © Stichting Concilium

English translations copyright © 2004 SCM-Canterbury Press Ltd

ISBN 0 334 03081 1

Printed by Biddles Ltd, King's Lynn

Concilium Published February, April, June, October
December

Contents

Introduction: This World can be Different[1]

LUIZ CARLOS SUSIN

'A different world is possible!' resounded from the loudspeakers on the balcony above the grass esplanade on which the crowd was gathered, next to the abundant river Guaíba, as the summer sun was setting. This proclamation, that 'a different world is possible', opened the second meeting of the World Social Forum, held in January 2002 in the city of Porto Alegre, the capital of Rio Grande do Sul, the southernmost state of Brazil, with some 1.4 million inhabitants. And so, in that opening ceremony with its staging and symbols, was born the slogan that has guided new meetings of the World Social Forum towards a utopian viewpoint capable of drawing together increasing numbers of people from all continents, coming from hundreds of social movements and NGOs, in one great movement aimed at a future world. The slogan 'A different world is possible' is not yet a motto for a set of orders, nor does it point to a course of action or militancy; it simply indicates a horizon or a time that is largely concerned with hope and with eschatology.

'But it is not another world beyond this one. A different world is possible here, on this planet earth,' the various speakers continued to tell the crowd. What would Popper or Marcuse or the critics of modern ideologies make of such statements? And what would Thomas More and the missionaries setting out for the New World in their caravels to found a new Christendom feel about them? What is certain is that anyone in that crowd who was familiar with theology must have wondered: Is this a millenialist, messianic utopia?

The great questions for millenialist dreams were: Who would the Messiah be and what would he do? Who would now be the one anointed to usher in the happy era of this different world? What needed to be done? And how should it be done? Does the church, the 'universal sacrament of salvation' (LG 1), still have anything to do with all this? On the esplanade that summer evening were many people from various churches, including bishops, but they were simply immersed in the spirit of the crowd. In a more intensely globalized world, in the 'global village', can religions play a transforming role through their potential for beliefs, dreams and ethics? Among the festive colours of that crowd on the riverbank, one could see various traditional religious garbs mixed in with the light and informal summer clothing. There were young people and adults, with different attitudes to religious faith or to expressions of their other choices, but they were all together on that esplanade, ready to accept the differing ways of building the common dream of 'a different possible world'.

There was, then, in this multitude of persons and of movements, a striking cultural and religious pluralism, coming together in a great movement towards a different world, or, more precisely, towards this world being different, qualitatively different. Was this a pluralist millennialism, a collective messianism, woven out of this convergence of social movements, of organizations, of human energies directed to a common endeavour? Was it a militant drive for a world developing into a democratic and pluralist socialism, an antidote to both the evil of free-market capitalism and the deservedly failed dictatorial socialism? We still need to ask the question when confronted with this fine utopian and milleniarist horizon – still extremely open and too general: Is a different world possible?[2]

There are many remaining questions and no complete answer. We are still learning that 'movements' make the flow of history but are by their nature ephemeral. And so they should be. Once their mission is accomplished, they naturally dissolve. Their institutionalization is a foretaste of their death-throes, the crucifixion of the Messiah. This has perhaps been the course of base church communities in Latin America, a mixture of movement and ecclesial structure. Lately the structure has been strengthened and the movement strangled. In the World Social Forum we have also seen the danger that NGOs will eventually take over and throttle the social movements, the apple of the Forum's eye, the stream that makes possible its existence and lends plausibility to its slogan of a different possible world.[3]

Analyses of the relationship between movement and institution often come to the opposite conclusion: precisely because intuition, movement and mysticism are ephemeral, they have to be underpinned with organization, with institutionalization. Marriage is the stabilization and protection of love. But it is also often at risk of becoming the tomb of love. How can the institution go on inspiring the original intuition and the early love? Churches and religions are institutions, vessels of clay that pour out but also contain the precious liquid of mysticism, of messianism, of the spirituality with the potential to change the world. Left to their own inertia, churches and religions crucify and bury messianic energies under their institutional weight. These energies, however, often in their very ups and downs, provide a powerful channel for the flow of spirituality that has the power to help this world and to stimulate social reform movements by infusing them with an unequalled mysticism, a generosity with no bounds, even of martyrdom. One of the great concerns of liberation theology, officially consecrated in the title of the 1968 Medellín document, 'The Presence of the Church in the Present-day Transformation of Latin America', is that living faith and religious practice should not necessarily be alienating or conservative but can also be revolutionary, transformative, opening up possibilities for making a different world achievable.

What sort of different world is possible? We all want, and in the end always will want, peace and justice, tranquillity and prosperity – for all. Today, however, these messianic benefits are conditioned by the sustainability and by the political and economic, technological and scientific, resources of a globalized world paradoxically ever more limited by the very course of its own development. In other words, if this world is to be sustainable, it must necessarily become 'different'. The prime sustainability is at once ecological and ethical. Above all, it requires an ethic of living together in peace and keeping the earth habitable, which means an ethic of pluralism and justice. Do religion, spirituality and theology possess resources to assist in the ecological and ethical sustainability of this world, helping it to become different? Perhaps the relevance of religions and churches depends on the answer to this question. If theology has nothing relevant to say on this sustainability, it had better remain silent. And it would be shameful for it to make its own *apologia*, to declare itself relevant *a priori*. The World Social Forum, with its utopian outlook and its stream of movements, could be a broad and suitable authority for judging and making a case for the type of theology that helps to promote an ecologically sustainable world, with justice and peace for all. Could God, when all is said and done, want anything else for this world of ours?

Under the aegis of the World Social Forum and its slogan, 'a different world is possible', a World Forum of Theology and Liberation is taking place in January 2005, in the same city of Porto Alegre.[4] The objective is to bring together those theologians, men and women, from the various Christian traditions and from all continents, who are producing theology in contexts of initiatives, movements and organizations in search of justice, peace and freedom for the sons and daughters of God, including all creatures

on earth. The evangelization mandate is tuned with the slogan of the World
Social Forum and becomes an imperative, for theology too: *this world can
and must be different*. Christian theology cannot remain cynically seated in
the square on the pretext that no one has summoned it to the task, nor can it
go and care for its own ecclesiastical oxen, consuming itself in concerns for
its own patch, its own space and its own rules, with its own identity and its
own self-justification, and absent itself from interpretation of and celebra-
tion of hope in a different possible world. It has heard the good news and is
impelled to evangelize, to make its contribution, but without abdicating
from what has been familiar to it since birth: the messianic dream of the
coming kingdom of God. Because 'The lion has roared; who will not fear?
The Lord God has spoken; who can but prophesy?' (Amos 3.8).

This issue of *Concilium* shares in the same outlook and forms part of the
same stream of social movements. It has taken upon itself the task of working out the reasons for such a great clamour for a different world. Clearly, it
is working these out not univocally but from a variety of disciplines: in Part
I, it relies on the contributions of specialists in sociology and philosophy,
treating the need for 'a different world' from three angles: the dead-ends and
unsustainability of the decided courses of some aspects of economics, politics, and today's dominant ideologies; then it looks at sketches of, pointers to
and experiments in a different possible world by social movements with
viable alternatives; plus – which implicates theology more directly but also
more arduously – the possibility of utopias and their role and place in
committed efforts at changing the present world.

In the recent past *Concilium* has devoted several issues to consideration of
the problems and possibilities, sufferings and victims, risks and hopes that
permeate the economy, power structures, cultures and religions in the midst
of growing globalization. Utopia, after the death of ideologies, has also
begun to be re-considered by *Concilium*. Should it be that we ought to treat
the subject from another, more radical viewpoint, stated by the theologian
Juan Luis Ruiz de la Peña, of happy memory, that this is the time for the
death of utopias and for new possibilities for a renewed eschatology? How to
distinguish without separating? How to unite without confusing? Are we not
facing new forms of the paradox of the relationship between natural and
supernatural, grace and works, and so on? However one looks at it, there is
no possibility of being comprehensive in re-thinking utopia and eschatology
for this world, but this does not excuse us from yet another consideration.
Or from dreaming and expressing our hope, like the poet Oscar Campana,
quoted by the admirable bishop-poet Pedro Casaldáliga when he confessed

his passion for utopias by changing his *Doctor honoris causa* to *Doctor 'passionis' causa*:

> If there were no road to take us
> our hands would open one,
> and there would be room for children,
> for life and for truth;
> and this place would be for everyone,
> in justice and in freedom.
> If anyone is willing, let me know:
> two of us then will make a start. . . .

In Part II of this issue, like experts drawing on treasure-chests of things old and new, the contributors turn to the resources of the religious traditions, with emphasis on the biblical and Christian tradition, to see how religious practice can become different, starting from other people, from other creatures and from the courtesy and justice we owe to all that is different from ourselves. This is absolutely not a matter of apology for religions, but of how religious traditions, with their ethics and mysticism, with their theology and their poetry, their representations of the divine, of the Creator and creation, can provide an apology and sustainability for a 'different' world.

In Part III, realistic and practical in tone, we begin with the relevance of minority religious traditions to the sustainability of a globalized world. Further consideration is given to the contribution religious traditions can make to political and economic sustainability. Finally, a case study is provided in the form of the possibility of a peace process in the Middle East conflict between Israelis and Palestinians, a difficult but possible peace and one of the test-cases for humankind to make 'a different world possible'.

Under the eschatological veil of life in abundance and looking towards the utopian horizon of a possible different world, *Concilium* joins in the stream of regional and global social movements in *exodus*, in the hope of *eis-odos*, of entry into a different world – this has to be possible. But, along with everything that is divine creation, it also depends on human decisions and responsibilities. Jon Sobrino concludes this interdisciplinary collection with a recollection of Ignacio Ellacuría, a contemporary martyr who, with clarity and faithful love, left the testimony that unachievable utopia can inspire and invigorate what can be achieved towards a world of justice and peace.

Translated by Paul Burns

Notes

1. An editorial decision has been made to prefer 'different' to 'other' in English, to avoid confusion with the 'other' world 'beyond' – a meaning ruled out in para. 2 below (*Trans.*)
2. The *Revista de Análises y Reflexión Teológica 'Alternativas'* (Managua) reacted immediately, in its January–June 2002 number, making this its general title, but with a question mark at the end.
3. The World Social Forum came into being, in fact, as a counterweight to the World Economic Forum held at Davos in Switzerland. This is why it takes place on the same dates. But it grew to such an extent that it outgrew its original intentions and developed surprising forms.
4. More information of the World Forum of Liberation and Theology can be found at www.pucrs.br/pastoral/fmtl.

I. Towards a Different World

The End of Neo-Liberalism, Unsustainable Capitalism, and the Need for a New Utopia

WIM DIERCKXSENS

We are faced with a situation in which sustained growth in the world economy no longer seems an obvious reality. For the first time since the 1930s we are looking at the possibility of a global recession with all the indicators for becoming a global depression. Capital accumulation is possible only as long as there is economic growth. Progress and economic growth turn out to be synonymous. Accumulating capital without economic growth is possible only by concentrating revenues. This cannot be a sustainable project in the long term, since its ultimate result will be economic contraction, meaning recession. Going against economic growth means, therefore, going against the very nature of capital, and so is a perverse option. This also produces the postulate that without economic growth, the standard of living will decline. From this viewpoint, standard of living is measured essentially by growth of Gross Domestic Product (GDP). All other indicators of human development are considered secondary. If growth proves negative there is recession, and if this lasts several years we speak of depression. Without solving the crisis, the very logic of the system would move into crisis. In my view, we have reached the limits of the possible in quantitative growth. The next world recession will have no solution, and this posits the need for and possibility of forming an alternative.

I. The threat of a world recession with no solution

After decades of an economic policy focussed on accumulation of capital through economic growth, neo-liberalism, since the 1970s but more so since the 1980s, has sought the growth of transnational and financial capital at the expense of revenue concentration and to the detriment of national and local markets throughout the world. This model of neo-liberal accumulation is known as globalization. This is a matter of economic war waged on existing

markets in the interests of transnational businesses. This policy has led to
the exclusion, increased labour exploitation, and expropriation of peripheral
economies. This process of accumulation based on concentration of wealth
is not sustainable.

The process of appropriating existing revenues and markets is taking
place to the detriment of economic growth. Since the 1970s the economic
war for markets has sapped the strength of the economic dynamism of the
periphery. The lost decades in Latin America since the 1980s, stemming
from the crisis of external debt, is a clear sign of this. The loss of economic
dynamism in the countries making the change from socialism to capitalism
has no precedent in history. Russian GDP, for example, in 1998 was less
than half what it had been in 1989. The currency destabilization in the so-
called 'Asiatic Tigers' caused a severe recession in that region, from which it
has not fully recovered.

Concentration of markets and of global revenue in fewer hands has
enabled the transnationals to maintain their profits but has lowered demand
for goods and services by the vast majority of people. It now threatens
growth in the major powers themselves. With the specific announcement of
simultaneous recession in the US, Europe and Japan at the end of 2001, the
sharing out of the global market and revenues reached its limit. Sharing out
declining global revenue does nothing but aggravate the world recession.
The growth of some countries at the expense of others is not a permanent
way out. This *sauve qui peut* approach will deepen the world recession and in
the long run not save anyone. The world recession will not only be more
synchronized than ever, but it will also cover greater parts of the world. A
recession with these characteristics will last for years and lead to a new
world depression. Neo-liberal economists do not understand the causes of
recession and persist in the most aggressive free-market policies.

II. Towards a simultaneous recession worldwide

This is not the first time the world economy has moved into recession. Such
cyclical crises have been observable since 1820. Less common and more
recent in the history of capitalism is the fact that cycles in individual
countries are tending to coincide more owing to the internationalization of
the economy. Recessions are tending to become both deeper and more widespread. In the 1920s Kondratieff identified periods of depression occurring
every fifty years. In these long cycles, upturns are characterized by increased
rates of earnings, downturns by a fall in rates of profit. A fresh increase in

profits would come from a new technological revolution, while each period of downturn is the product of its now generalized application.

In this scheme, it seems that economic cycles will always recur. This makes capitalism seem capable of emerging from every crisis, on the strength of yet another technological innovation. So the continuing expectation is that a new wave of technological innovation will save rates of return and so capitalism itself in each recession. The paradox, however, is that we have reached such a rate of technological replacement that the average lifespan of a given technology is virtually nil ('software' being a good example of this). Shortening technological life even further would be counterproductive for capitalism. The speed of technological change has an inbuilt production cost that is no longer balanced by the reduction in unit cost that makes the innovation possible. The result of this is that profit rates, instead of rising, tend to decrease owing to the speed of technological change. With a lowering of gross earnings in the manufacturing sector, capital no longer seeks to grow through economic growth but on the basis of the concentration of existing earnings. Periods in which capital accumulation is based at times on growth and at others on the concentration of already existing markets and earnings reflect the great economic cycles.

The first cycle, from 1780 to 1847, was due to the Industrial Revolution in England; the second, from 1847 to 1890, to the generalized use of steam power; the third, from 1890 to 1939, to the generalized use of the electric motor and the internal combustion engine. The fourth cycle of expansion began in 1948, peaking towards the end of the 1960s, with a still unknown period of decline. This cycle is attributable to the generalized use of electronics and atomic energy. It was hoped that the last phase of decline, started at the end of the 1960s, would be halted in the 1990s with the application of computing and IT technology. Instead of this happening, gross profit rates fell even further in the manufacturing sector, leaving the economists to resolve the paradox.

Maddison has analyzed the internationalization of the economic recession in historical terms. It was not until the end of the nineteenth century that the first international recession appeared, affecting a third of the central powers but lasting only a year. The economic recession in World War I affected 50 per cent of these countries. The Great World Depression of the 1930s affected 75 per cent of the major powers and for the first time in the history of capitalism lasted for more than three years, from which it got its name of 'great world' depression. As national recessions are synchronized, the falls in growth rates for the economies affected tend to become steeper. At the end of the nineteenth century the lowest point of growth for the sixteen central countries scarcely reached minus 1 per cent; during the First World War period this was minus 5 per cent; in the Great Depression of the 1930s minus 6.5 per cent; and in the 1945–6 recession it reached minus 11 per cent, breaking all historical moulds.

The tendencies of the past allow us to make projections for the future. A recession in a globalized world tends to be more extensive in reach and more synchronized in time than ever before. Between 1948 and 1973 we saw a cycle of economic expansion on a world scale. Growth rates of Gross World Product were high and sustained and spread widely across the globe. Beginning in 1973, the annual growth rate on a world scale began gradually to decline. The start of the new millennium produced a worldwide recession on a scale not seen since the 1930s. The majority of the central economies found themselves threatened with recession. Accumulation of capital based on economic growth came to a complete halt, while accumulation based on concentration of wealth came up against definite obstacles. The economic recession produced a crisis for transnational and financial capital itself. A generalized stock-exchange crisis is in progress, with failures of large businesses and banks in prospect. In brief, there are all the signs of a new world depression.

III. The unsustainable nature of neo-liberalism

With a new world depression, apparently broader and deeper than any previous, on the horizon, without conditions for a fresh boost to economic growth, there will be no way out except a change of economic system. Diverting investment from the speculative, redistributive, and non-productive spheres through measures that impose taxes on currency specu-lations (such as the Tobin tax) is a necessary but insufficient condition. Without an increase in the rate of return in the manufacturing sector itself, there will be no fresh flow of capital towards that sector. This is the scenario economists are least able to understand. They cannot see the difference between productive and unproductive investment other than the profit to be made from it. The economic recession itself will show that it is not the same to make profits from a process of concentrating wealth as it is to increase earnings from the manufacturing sector. Accumulation on the basis of the first process leads inevitably to a contraction of the economy, while accumu-lation on the basis of production increases this and proves more sustainable.

Accumulation on the basis of concentrating revenue consists essentially in making money with money without increasing real wealth. The profit obtained is derived not from an increase in existing wealth but from its re-distribution. The most profitable means are by speculation on the stock and currency markets. This form of non-productive accumulation developed during the 1970s with the rejection of the Keynesian principles embodied in the Welfare State. During the post-war period, investment was closely tied to the production process through a whole battery of economic regulations. The descending rate of profit from manufacturing towards the end of the 1970s gave rise to neo-liberalism, which freed movement of capital from these restraints.

On the international level, private banks began to grant loans without any ties to manufacturing processes. This practice led, for example, to the external debt incurred by Latin America in particular and the countries of the periphery in general. This was the basis for the external debt and the cause of their crisis. Then the policies of structural adjustment encouraged the substitution of national markets by international ones, the replacement of state enterprises by multinationals, the acquisition of local businesses, their merger with multinational corporations, and currency speculation by peripheral countries. All these investments did not generate new wealth, did not enlarge the total market, did not encourage growth but promoted the re-distribution of the world's existing goods and markets. In the midst of the resulting economic stagnation, the multinationals prospered. Wagers on these winners then increased stock-market speculation.

Accumulation based on concentration of revenue decreases global con-sumption. The more fortunate consume, percentage-wise, less of their income than the poorest. Concentration of revenue means a contraction in global demand and so saps economic growth. Carrying on with accumula-tion based on the same model in more aggressive form provokes a downward spiral in economic growth leading to a world recession. The lesson is clear: we have to return to growth, or the very rationale of capitalism will find itself in crisis.

IV. Falling productivity in the technological era: an insoluble dilemma for capitalism

Under the capitalist system economic production develops in a competitive milieu, designed to maximize profit. Having access to the latest technology means enjoying competitive advantages in order to maximize profit. Tech-nological innovation in itself, however, does not guarantee a higher rate of profit. The profitability of technological innovation depends on the cost of its replacement. The ability of a business to increase production through the latest technology will, on principle, ensure its competitiveness. The more technological innovation is stimulated, however, the shorter its useful life and so the greater the cost of replacing it. Once the cost of technological replacement exceeds the reduction in labour cost brought about by this replacement, the profit rate, instead of rising, tends to fall. It is as though the productivity (profitability) of labour had not increased.

The period of rapid post-war economic growth was stimulated by a methodical shortening of the useful life of products and of technology. By this means there was a return to quicker profits. The result was the consumer and exploiter society, with an increasing cost to nature, the environment, and life itself. Life itself was subordinated to the economic rationale, not the other way round. Ever more rapid and sophisticated technological replacement, however, increases the cost of innovation. The final outcome is as though productivity (profitability) has decreased. Capital then tends to abandon the manufacturing sector, with resulting unemployment. In such circumstances, wages are lowered, working hours are increased, and work is intensified. So the rate of profit increases alongside increasing exploitation of the workforce.

Between 1950 and 1973 there was ever faster technological replacement. This was reflected in a decrease in the average lifespan of technology. In the G7 countries the average lifespan of buildings and equipment dropped from 15.7 to 10.1 years, a reduction of 35 per cent. As the rate of technological replacement increases, so the cost of replacement tends to increase faster than the savings in production costs achieved by innovation. And so the profit rate falls. The gross profit of non-financial enterprises in the US varied in the period 1950 to 1970 between 15 and 20 per cent of (non-financial) GDP; between 1970 and 1990 it was around 10 per cent, falling to a mere 7.5 per cent in 2001. The response of major capital to the tendency to lower profits has been to abandon investment in the manufacturing sector and turn to redistributive and speculative, meaning non-productive sectors. As a result, since 1973 there has been a fall in growth of investment in machinery from 4.8 per cent between 1950 and 1973 to 3.5 per cent between 1973 and 1987. Over the same period there was a prolongation of the average lifespan of technology from 10.1 to 12.9 years. This is explained by a wider application of the system of patents.

From 1991 to 1997, in the age of computation and communication, investment in machinery and equipment began to grow once more, particularly in the United States. The development of this new technology produced enormous benefits for its productive sectors. But when this new technology was applied to other economic sectors and not least to the financial sector, the results in productivity terms were disappointing. What happened? The average lifespan of technology became shorter than ever and the speed of technological replacement became higher than ever. The average lifespan of buildings and equipment reduced in the US from 14 to 7 years between 1987 and the end of the 1990s. In Japan its lifespan came down from 11 to 5 years. This seems to mark the limits of what is possible in technological replacement.

Most productive sectors seem to be showing, to a greater degree than ever before, the same dilemma of the negative profitability of technological replacement. As the costs of this rise more rapidly than the savings they produce in production costs, the benefits vanish, and the whole situation becomes as though there had been no increase in productivity. This is the paradox of lost productivity in the era of the new technology. In the G7 countries productivity increased between 1960 and 1967 at an annual rate of 4.3 per cent; between 1979 and 1989 this decreased to 1.7 per cent; between 1989 and 1994 it reduced further to 1.2 per cent, and in the second half of the 1990s it disappeared altogether. This tendency was most marked in the United States. We had reached the limits of the possible in shortening the useful life of technology, and with it the limits of the possibility of linking investment to production under the capitalist system.

V. The need for alternatives to neo-liberalism

(a) A Noah's ark with no space

Economists usually express the productivity of labour in terms of an hourly rate. In an open economy, this is influenced by external transfers of values. In a situation where the rate of economic growth is falling, the redistribution of wealth among nations seems to offer a solution. The South–North transfer has become more acute under neo-liberalism. Between 1985 and 1995 the hundred poorest countries saw their GDP per person fall by almost 15 per cent, while at the same time the GDP of the G7 countries rose by 22 per cent. This transfer inflated the GDP of the G7 and thereby made it possible for them to underestimate their loss of productivity through technological replacement.

Towards the end of the 1990s the incomes of the 300 richest people in the world exceeded the incomes of the 2 million poorest. In the struggle for global markets, 200 multinationals increased their share of Gross World Product from 17 per cent in 1965 to over 35 per cent by the end of the century, while all multinationals accounted for over 50 per cent. In this economic battle for market share, however, the rate of economic growth has not stopped declining. The triumphalism of the most powerful capitalist entities in the midst of a world of losers has increased the value of their shares on the stock market. Positing a perpetual increase in their share value supposes a perpetually increasing concentration of wealth. This supposition can be seen to be absurd in the context of a coming worldwide recession. With the world market divided among ever fewer multinationals, the renewed parcelling-out of the existing market becomes more disputed, still more so when this market is recoiling under the impact of a drop in global demand. Sales contract and profits fall with them. A financial crisis inevitably follows. It is possible to postpone this crisis in individual nations, but this implies taking more than economic steps. The war for markets becomes total.

(b) A sinking Noah's ark

The continued division of the world market will not offer a solution for all transnational capital. The war for the world market requires more than economic means if it is to be won. This implies a threat of war on a global scale. The war on terrorism declared by the US after 11 September 2001 has no visible enemy or clear aim. Its essence is that, in the name of a conflict of civilizations, Western and above all US capital should save itself at the expense of other civilizations. The East will be excluded in order to save the West, and within the West the US is singled out as the 'chosen nation'. Within this scenario, multilateral negotiations are reopened. Faced with the threat of war, multilateral agreements have to favour the unilateral interests of the United States. This is true on a world scale of the WTO Ministerial held in Qatar in 2001 and on a continental scale of the Free Trade Area of the Americas.

The profit forecasts of the multinationals improved. Their share prices on the Dow Jones index increased to the point where at the start of 2002 they had surpassed the levels of the day before 9/11. This did not happen in Europe, where share prices remained below the levels of 10 September 2001. Still less did it happen in Japan, where the recession continues, or in most nations of the periphery. The New York stock market recovered thanks to the flight of international capital there, not because of the economic dynamism of the US, but because of low expectations in the rest of the world. This is a new speculative shift with no other possible outcome than its collapse in the medium term. In a war for global markets waged basically for the sake of the capital of a single nation, ever more countries will be forced into recession. No nation can in fact escape this, not even the winner, which will have destroyed the trading partners on which it depends. Short-term triumph means a deeper recession in the long term.

The increase in defence spending as a percentage of GNP planned by the US over the coming years is not sufficient to boost internal demand. It will benefit the multinationals linked to the military-industrial complex. Its positive effect on share prices on the New York market is based on expectations of future demand and not a real resurgence. Raising defence spending even further will mean higher interest rates. This will endanger demand for consumer durables, a demand that reactivated credit buying up to mid-2004, and deplete Federal Reserve funds in order to prop up the stock market. In the short term, military spending increases demand and production. In the medium term its products do not fit into the civilian economy, which loses even more dynamism. It then becomes essential to sell arms in order to shift their unproductive cost on to other nations so as not to affect the civilian economy of the United States. The more one-sided the war becomes, the harder it will be to shift defence expenditure on to other nations. Such a shift was plausible in the context of the Cold War. A unilateral war against terrorism reduces this capacity. It will therefore have an adverse effect on the civilian economy of the United States.

The indirect effect of technological inventions on the increase in productivity in the civilian sphere is the next legitimation. Computers and IT derive from the industrial-military complex. Their introduction into civilian economies has accelerated the negative effect on productivity. The idea that a war-based economy can be of benefit to civilian economy in the future is therefore false. An eventual massive destruction of buildings and equipment in a future war and their re-building at high profit margins is another mirage. Reconstruction will always have to face the dilemma of low profit margins in the manufacturing sphere and so provides no solution for triumphant high capitalism.

VI. The global crisis of legitimacy: the need for another rationale

It is a question of time before the recession affects the whole world through a stock-market collapse. Business bankruptcies in the US in 2001 were three times the number they were in the late 1990s. We have seen the first bankruptcies of large multinationals: the cases of Enron and World.Com in the US and more recently of Parmalat in Italy are just the tip of the iceberg that can be expected. With the start of a world recession, imports by the North will decrease in volume and in price. This will deprive the nations of the South of any ability to repay their external debt. They will have no alternative but to use the funds to boost their internal markets. Argentina is a pointer to this tendency. This process will prevent a deeper implantation of neo-liberalism. In this way aggressive neo-liberalism leads to its own opposite. In the midst of a world recession, *sauve qui peut* will generate protectionism on all sides. The US, the 'chosen nation', itself provided an example of this with its protection of its steel industry through tariffs on imports. Nevertheless, it continues to preach the doctrine of free trade to the rest of the world. Its action produced counter-measures in other developed nations, and this climate led to failures of multilateral negotiations, as happened to the WTO.

So the crisis of neo-liberalism will engender protectionism and nationalism, and this tendency will affect transnational sales. This is turn will accentuate world recession and international stock-market and financial collapse. *Sauve qui peut* may encourage more bellicose attitudes. A battle for markets waged on an all-out *sauve qui peut* basis will result in no one being saved. In Beinstein's phrase, we have entered the phase of 'senile capitalism'. This situation and its accompanying pain will give birth to a new understanding that without providing space for the development of local and national economies there will be no solution for anyone. An alternative thus becomes not only possible but necessary.

An alternative proposal becomes more strategic to the extent that it focusses on the basic contradiction in the existing scheme of things. Being able to steer alternatives towards the basic contradiction in the short and medium term requires it to become visible. The basic contradiction in the existing scheme is that capitalism has reached a moment in history when it has become impossible to tie investment to production with profitable results. Further development of productive processes, in other words, is no longer possible under existing economic regimes and social relationships. This contradiction will become visible in the frustration of processes designed to resolve it.

World capital is conscious of the contradiction and has tried to solve it by looking for increased state subsidies, amongst other measures, to reduce the costs of technological innovation. At the same time, patents policy means the simultaneous privatization of its benefits on a long-term basis. Patents policy produces highly protectionist economic measures designed to favour multinational businesses. This protectionist solution works in the short term but fails to resolve the basic contradiction in the medium term; on the contrary, it further aggravates it. Patents policy works as a substitute for markets without patents, bringing about a private monopoly of rights to intellectual property. This policy accentuates the concentration of existing markets and income streams and contracts the market economy as a whole. This way of prolonging the average lifespan of technology worsens, in other words, economic recession on a global scale. The result is relative over-production and under-consumption, with a resulting fall in rates of profit and so deepening recession.

If we are to pull back from world recession, there is no alternative but to return to the link between investment and production and to aim for global demand through a more equitable distribution of income throughout the world. At first sight this might appear to be a neo-Keynesian solution on a world scale. This would, however come up against the dilemma of the limit reached by technological replacement on a profitable basis. The paradox of a crisis of productivity being brought about by technological innovation can be resolved only by a planned regulation of the average lifespan of tech-nology, reducing the pace of replacement in the central economies and at the same time declaring intellectual property a world patrimony.

Worldwide regulation of the pace of technological replacement and decla-ration of knowledge a world patrimony, however, means placing limits on the very possibilities of competition among individual businesses. The engine of the market economy, knowledge, would be subordinate to the common good, rather than the other way round. In this case we would be dealing with a sort of reverse Keynesianism: the average lifespan of tech-nology would be prolonged. This will produce a rapid decline in demand for technology and equipment in the North. To prevent capital being devalued as capital, the money released in the North will flow toward the South. With the socialization of knowledge and North-South capital flows, the structural bases of unequal development between North and South will soon be removed. Competition through competitive prices resulting from different technologies will rapidly be levelled out. Competition will be forced to base itself on more on the quality of a product and less on its price, which will tend to even out.

Standard of living assessed in monetary terms will thereby lose its mean-ing, and it will be measured more by the quality of products and their longevity. In this way economic growth, in money terms, will be subordinate to the genuine standard of living. This investment in economic reason will allow the economy to function for the sake of life itself and not the other way round. Prolonging the useful life of products in general will liberate natural and economic resources in the North (for which 80 per cent of them are destined) without any loss of genuine standard of living. With products designed for maximum use, their quality and lifespan will improve. Production will gradually come to be defined in relation to real needs instead of creating needs for the sake of selling goods to meet them. In this way production priorities will, over time, come to be defined from the viewpoint of the actual users. This will mean a decentralization in production policy: what is produced and where it is produced will depend on local and national needs and specialities and no longer in the final analysis on the private interests of a few multinational businesses.

The reversal of priorities toward the quality of the product will set limits to consumerism and to the seduction of consumers for the sake of increased sales. In this way we can achieve an increase in the genuine standard of living of the North together with negative economic growth. With the liberation of natural resources and money, we shall at the same time be able to achieve an unprecedented development of genuine standard of living in the South. Genuine development there will, for a time, be accompanied by economic development, but so long as the liberation of natural resources and money in the North exceeds their investment in the South, it will be possible to achieve greater conservation of the environment at the same time.

In this context, what is surplus, in relative terms, is money in the North. The excess of money in the North will lose its value of use as a means of exchange. In order not to lose its future acquisitive capacity, it will need to flow towards the South, where it will increase wealth even in terms of value. If the growth in wealth in the South is slower than the deceleration of the economy in the North, affluence will tend to result even with negative rates of interest. With an increase in genuine development in the North with decreasing amounts of money, money itself will lose its use value. The engine of the economy of the future will cease to be capital: from then on the new 'capital' will be knowledge, and this will be universalized and cease to be a scarce commodity. This looks like utopia today, but tomorrow it could be reality.

Translated by Paul Burns

Different Worlds from the Viewpoint of Planetary Citizenship

CÂNDIDO GRZYBOWSKI

The World Social Forum (WSF) is one of those events that demarcate epochs. They have a 'before them' and an 'after them'. They seem to arise unexpectedly, but as they turn out to be pointers to both ends and beginnings, people discover that everything was ripe for their appearance, that history was ready to bring them forth, so to speak. The WSF took shape as an antithesis to globalized capitalism, to the law of the free market in the service of great corporations, to the logic of terrorism and war, to imperialism. It seeks to globalize humankind, on the foundation of solidarity among the poor, in a logic based on human rights and peace.

The first WSF was held in Porto Alegre in 2001, as a counterweight to the World Economic Forum in Davos, then in its thirtieth year. It provoked such a swell of imagination and dreams that by its second session, in 2002, again in Porto Alegre, it was clear that we had laid the foundations of a powerful movement of opinion-forming, capable of gathering everything and everyone under the slogan, 'A different world is possible'. We created forums of every sort – regional, thematic, local – and the swell has only become bigger from this beginning. We held the third WSF also in Porto Alegre in 2003, and then we daringly went to Mumbai (Bombay) in India in 2004, giving the Forum an unquestionably universal presence. The energy generated by the process has continued to expand and to bring fresh challenges. We are returning to Porto Alegre in 2005, with the task of making new qualitative leaps in political mobilization and intervention, proving our vitality in the framework of the prevailing (dis)order.

What, though, is being produced in this factory of ideas at the base of the WSF? What does it possess that is so fundamental as to enable it to be taken as marking a new era, if not in human history as a whole, at least in the time-frame of a generation? Perhaps the best reply is that the WSF has to be seen as the creation of something truly human by a whole mass of people who believe themselves to be contributing to the fashioning of their world, to be giving meaning and purpose to their lives and the course they take. Basically, allowing us to dream and to adopt an active stance is the WSF's most revolutionary act, at a time when the ideology of one way of thinking and the non-viability of other alternatives (the 'end of history') seemed to have been definitively established. The WSF is, essentially, an act of freedom, a way of seeking to return to the exercise of freedom to think of and imagine different possible worlds.

My aim here is to provide a view of, a glance at, the WSF. As a space for freedom, in which a variety of views cross and collide, held by a huge diversity of social agents with their multiplicity of involvements and identities – in the face of the unanimity and uniformity imposed by all-encompassing economic-financial globalization with its fundamentalisms – the Forum is bound to generate a great diversity of responses. This, though, is its novelty and its strength, the basis of a new political culture of citizenship. This makes the WSF a multi-faceted bloc, lending itself to various and contradictory readings, all of them legitimate.

I sincerely believe the WSF to be a great storehouse of alternatives. Nevertheless, rather than just alternatives as such, we need to look at the collision courses, the process by which alternatives emerge from confrontation and discussion, indicating possible agendas for change and democratization. In effect, the Forum takes shape among the joyful sound produced by belief in the capacity of everyone, men and women, making us value the contributions of all in terms of experiences and knowledge, by constituent citizenship in the sense of moulding economies and states, occupying existing spaces and opening up new spaces of recognition of human rights, generating a great wave of opinion, calling for a climate in which we can think differently and with the possibility of differing.

The WSF is simply a forum for people to meet each other, a fermenting agent for transforming all its participants, an act of hope. Alternatives effectively take shape under the inspiration of the Forum, but adapted to the various conditions and possibilities that we ourselves develop, in a world rich in its natural and human diversity.

I. Collective agents – builders of alternatives

The WSF cannot be dissociated from the political emergence of citizenship on a planetary scale. In it the most diverse social movements and organizations in terms of geography, nationality and culture, all affirming their universality as upholders of common rights by virtue of the specificity of the relationships and structures of which they form part and the conditions under which they live, all converge. The WSF is forged as a bloc of collective agents, all bearing different socio-cultural and political identities but fused together by their common consciousness of humanity and citizenship.

Rather than creating alternatives, the WSF acts as a powerful movement bringing together those who build alternatives to make different worlds possible. It is not the WSF that creates collective agents. What the Forum actually does is to deepen what is already emerging from struggles against the ruling globalization, its agents, institutions and policies. Here it is worth noting in particular the process of struggles against the global institutions and the policies they propagate.

The memorable days in Seattle, in late 1999, when the WTO negotiations were paralysed by the work of a mega-coalition of movements and organizations, are one example. We also have the whole mobilization against the World Bank and the IMF, culminating in the establishment of the world Jubilee network against external debt, and the periodical mobilizations to coincide with G8 summits. There was also the whole process of mobilization and active participation in connection with the cycle of UN Conferences beginning with the Rio 'Earth Summit' in 1992 and extending throughout the last decade of the twentieth century.

The WSF has grown from the belly of this process and given it new meaning, permitting the effective development of citizenship on a planetary scale. Mobilizations such as those of 15 February 2003, when millions took to the streets in cities all over the world, in a concerted movement of protest against the imminent imperialist invasion of Iraq and in favour of world peace, would not be possible without the common reference point of the WSF.

The WSF nourishes and strengthens the birth of a new citizenship, capable of forging a different world, by making its central concern the common consciousness of humanity and of the heritage we all hold in common. The participation of the most diverse social agents, with the plurality of their visions and choices, gives the WSF vitality and becomes the basis of a new political culture. It brings with it an understanding of equality in difference, of differences with the same rights, of affirmation of one's own identity in the discovery and recognition of the identity of others, of the importance and power of everyone and of all at once, without predominance or fundamentalism of any kind. In this sense, the WSF is a practical and historical embodiment of the concept that we are all part of a same and common humanity. It also reaffirms the new understanding of the greater common good we hold in order to share and preserve. Earth with its resources, water, the sun, the atmosphere, biodiversity – everything, in effect, that guarantees life itself on this planet – are inseparable from human consciousness. The *no to the mercantilization of life and humanity* sets the boundaries of the new planetary citizenship, which is capable of building a different world.

This process is still marked by enormous contradictions and challenges. In the end, we come to the WSF laden with our own political practices and visions, our prejudices, racisms, Marxisms, fundamentalisms, all the product of life situations and daily confrontations in the place on the planet we inhabit. We are citizens of the world, but we have an address, a house, a place in our region and with our people. We are universal, but we have no way of losing our specificity and deep identification with our local culture and that of our group. Besides this, as we grow up we become imbued with the political cultures of our time and place. This makes the WSF a radical invitation to change ourselves and become citizens of the world, in order to universalize our understanding and vision, without losing our references. The challenge is of consequence, then, since, as women's movements rightly state in the their struggle against fundamentalisms, what is truly fundamental is people, and people are different within their equality. Self-reconstruction is a gigantic task for the WSF, in the sense of contributing to forge collective agencies to make different worlds possible.

A central task, as Boaventura Sousa Santos rightly states, is *translation*. We need to understand one another, not only in the technicality of language but also in what it represents by way of culture and identity, of ways of seeing and experiencing that, translated, nourish universality in diversity. It is a question of translating within social agencies, that is, within movements and organizations with the same purpose but deriving from different geo-graphical and cultural situations. And it is also a matter of translating between different social agencies, between movements and organizations that are different collective subjects. In this sense the WSF is an embryo of a civic pedagogy of a new type, of socio–cultural and political translation designed to forge a planetary citizenship. This is an enormous task and one that is of itself an alternative with which to confront the homogenizing world of globalization.

Another task for the emerging citizenship to be found in the WSF is the discovery or enablement of new forms of political practice that will value the horizontality of participation. Networks are not an invention of the WSF, but it cannot exist without them. The contribution the WSF can possibly make in the context of a new political culture is simply to deepen networked political action. The challenge here is to confront received ideas that dominate our left-wing political traditions. There is no more or less important agent, there is just the challenge to agree collective action among many, each dependent on the other. Networks are more than cobwebs; they are the practical expression of a citizenship that embraces the world across frontiers.

II. All human rights for all people: the guiding principle of alternatives

The WSF overturns the order of ruling theories, both the ideology that drives neo-liberal globalization and the political–ideological traditions of the Left. The primacy in building different worlds does not reside in the economy or the market or the state or the winning of political power. It lies in active citizenship. Citizenship needs the economy and the state, but it is what makes them. It is a matter of collective agents themselves reappropriating the making of the world, as holders of equal rights, without exclusions or discriminations. The WSF is an invitation to restate the participation of all as a condition of a different world. A different world will be made through our participation in the collective human adventure of democratic and sustainable appropriation and use of the resources of our common heritage, the planet, responsibly making our own impression on it in accordance with our needs, dreams and desires.

Once again, the WSF does not invent but deepens what is already there as an alternative. It is a matter of democracy understood as a process founded on a way of building the world, of producing the material and cultural conditions of life in the world, on the basis of the participation of all its inhabitants. The world will be inclusive if they all take part in its construction. We would share goods and services, would respect all identities and cultures, if we were all engaged in producing them. We would respect and preserve the common heritage we possess, if we could all feel dependent on it in order to live.

The WSF contributes to the rise of fresh alternatives, democratic, sustainable and diverse as we are and as the earth we possess is, by erecting common values and ethical principles on which democracy can be based as a way of living as a collective entity, as the basis for the means of forming the world. It means believing in the dream and the utopia of an ever more human world, one of rights and peace, without fundamentalisms or exclusions. But it also means a radical critique of the capitalist way of organizing and living in society. This is the capitalism that, in its globalized form, reveals its basic character of exploitation, concentration, destruction and exclusion. The challenge for the WSF is to deepen critique of capitalism so as to be capable of contributing to the building of alternatives that will be transforming in the sense of generating more human, just, supportive, democratic and sustainable societies.

The WSF has raised the collective right to development of every people and of all the peoples that form the human collectivity to the centre of the debate on alternatives. I understand the right to development as the creation of public space, of economic, political and cultural structures, relationships and processes, of laws and institutions, public works and policies favourable to the production of goods and services, by both public bodies and private agents, so as to guarantee the full enjoyment of human – civil and political, economic, social and cultural – rights by all the citizens of both genders who form a nation, in accordance with their needs and desires, based on their localities and their cultures. Therefore, the collective right to development, based on active participation, moulds alternative solutions to the building of society – democratic, sustainable and diverse, respectful of equality and social justice.

Models of development appropriate to what we are as human beings form the point of convergence and, at the same time, of the divergence that gives life to the debates within the WSF process. Models and solutions will necessarily be diverse, with a basis in respect for principles of a solid democracy rooted in solidarity and sustainability in the appropriation and use of the common heritage. Our debates lead us to move discussion to the local level, which is where active citizenship really counts. But we cannot prescind from consideration of a favourable international order that would act as a subsidiary guarantee, underpinning local exercise of the right to development belonging to each nation and every group of human beings on the planet.

The right to development is an affirmation of a share in the right to science, to technology, to knowledge, with communications systems and networks that socialize information without dominating. The right to development is a right to sovereignty and secure access to food and nutrition for every nation, as democratic and sustainable access to our collective natural heritage. The right to one's own identity and culture is a condition of the right to development. All this forms the underpinning of the amalgam of collective agents that confront one another, debate, converge and diverge within the process and space of the WSF, respecting and mutually strengthening one another as builders of different worlds, as an alternative to the destructive and exclusive homogenization of the economic–financial globalization and the warrior imperialism under which we still live.

III. Thinking the way to transforming action: the methodological challenge of the WSF

Many people hope and wish for the WSF to be what would be its own death: an organization that defines a project and the strategy everyone should pursue. As a Forum, it can only be a space for strategic thinking, of thinking as a way to action, but leaving the decision on what to do, how and with whom, to each of its agents, according to their own possibilities, conditions and wishes. In effect, the exercise of a participative method of thinking the way to action, respecting diversity and nourishing itself on it, is the central challenge for the WSF process. As long as it continues to renew itself in exercising freedom in thinking the way to transforming action, the WSF will continue to swell like a wave and to be a source of alternatives to the capitalist globalization that engulfs us and that generates war, concentration and exclusions throughout the world.

As a conclusion to my reflections here – themselves an act of free thinking in the spirit of the WSF – I should like to draw attention to the methodological question as the central political issue facing us as we think of alternatives and of different worlds. We have many gaps in our political culture, at the heart of our civil society, gaps that we need conscientiously to identify in order to fill them. The WSF can form a great sphere for innovating dialogue within and among its collective agents, developing methods that lead us into thinking and acting truly as citizens of the world. But to be able to do so, we need to be capable of mobilizing people across geographical boundaries to reach the different regions of the world and the countries in each, and across social and cultural barriers to reach the invisible members of society, those who are not organized or lack the resources to participate. We need to recognize how far we still are from expressing the diversity of world civil society and of those who compose it. We need, without any doubt, to be capable of finding inclusive methods of enabling us to go beyond the elites of organizations and establish dialogues that will translate from the top down and from the bottom up, among ourselves, recognizing that inequality determines what we are.

For the WSF of 2005, in Porto Alegre, we are trying to work out a method that will allow us to exercise internal democracy from the construction of our overall subject matter, what to discuss, to the sum total of activities, how to discuss them, and the programme itself, our collective programme of thinking the way to action. We are carrying out a broad process of consultation, so that everyone can tell the WSF what they want and what ideas and experiences, plans and results they can contribute. The collective and democratic appropriation of the act of planning the process and the event of the WSF is, in itself, an alternative way of beginning to think of different possible worlds. Our radicalness lies not only in the results we show but, first and foremost, in the way we achieve them.

This is the simplest and perhaps the most innovative message of the WSF. But we need to exercise solidarity among ourselves. The decision to create a great solidarity fund to enable some among us to support others with fewer resources, taking this upon ourselves as a collective responsibility, points in the same direction. We seek to practise what we preach. This gives the WSF the power to charge people's batteries, gives us the energy to dare and to begin the building of different worlds here and now. And, most importantly, we do all this with great happiness and enjoyment of life.

Translated by Paul Burns

Utopia Set Aside

If we are convinced that 'a different world is possible' and really want this 'different world' to become a reality, our first and most indispensable action has to be to regain a utopian consciousness. We need this because, as Max Horkheimer has rightly said, utopia represents on the one hand a critique of what exists and on the other a proposal for what should exist.[1] So, if we neither criticize the world we have nor make proposals for the world that should exist – that is, if our lives and plans are not guided by 'utopian reason' and its corresponding state of mind and way of thinking and of feeling – it will become clear that we are happy as we are, that we are satisfied with the present 'order', which has been imposed on us and accepted by us with pleasure. And then, logically, people satisfied with what they have cannot be expected to produce any sort of change. The 'satisfied' will always defend with tooth and claw the proposition that the best of all possible worlds is the one we are enjoying here and now.

Without any doubt, the greatest danger all of us face at the present time is that the 'satisfied' have the power and the means to impose on the 'global village' in which we all live what has most accurately been defined (by Franz Hinkelammert) as 'utopian ingenuousness'. The ingenuousness consists in ourselves adopting and forcing on others the utopia of 'a society that produces no more utopias'.[2] And this, unfortunately, is the state we have reached. Hardly anyone still thinks of utopias, because we have almost all had our heads filled with the notion that the market economy is the only economy, to which 'there is no alternative',[3] and have assimilated it into the very marrow of our most cherished ideas. And, as is to be expected from people who think and live like this, speaking of utopia is seen as speaking of a real extravagance. Utopia has thus been itself removed to the sidelines, to the realm of exclusion, of extravagance. Under such conditions, speaking seriously of the possibility of a 'different world' is more than a difficult task; it is virtually impossible. How has this situation come about, and is there any way out of it?

I. The failure of utopias

In 1947, two years after the end of the Second World War, Karl Popper wrote: 'I consider what I call utopianism an attractive theory, and even an enormously attractive one, but I also consider it dangerous and pernicious. I believe it is self-defeating and that it leads to violence.'[4] I am not concerned here with examining the basic reasons that led Popper to adopt such a decidedly anti-utopian stance. He clearly had his reasons for writing what he did when he did. The utopia of Communism as it had developed in the Soviet Union and the nihilistic Nietzschean utopia promoted by Nazism had produced many millions of innocent victims. What Popper could not foresee in 1947 was that 'the open society', which he put forward as the ideal, was going to develop (in fact) into the neo-liberal form of global market, generating more self-defeat and more violence than Stalin's Communism or Hitler's Nazism. The fact is that we now know that because of the growing concentration of wealth produced by the global market, neo-liberal capitalism is causing more than 70,000 deaths every day from hunger, malnutrition and their resulting pandemics. These figures are given by the annual UN Reports on Human Development. Neither Hitler nor Stalin, for all their barbarity, achieved such levels of brutality and violence.

There is no doubt that the three great utopias of the twentieth century promised us a better world. But historical experience has shown us that these three utopias have resulted in the most violent and most frustrating century in the whole of human history. Among other reasons for this is that these three utopias have not allowed even the minimum of criticism of the project that each of them has offered us. The fact is that these three utopias have ended by being, *de facto*, three agents of a violence that has gone beyond the limits of anything human beings could have imagined.

Why has this happened? In the first place, because none of the three utopias mentioned has been a utopia properly so called, if we give the word 'utopia' the meaning generally assigned to it. This is because one constituent element of a utopia, as I have said, is critique of what exists. But neither Stalinist Communism, nor Hitlerian Nazism, nor neo-liberal capitalism has allowed a radical critique of its systems. This is obvious in the case of Stalin's Communism and Hitler's Nazism, because both were totalitarian systems. When we come to neo-liberalist capitalism, however, the case is not so clear, since – at least at first sight – the capitalist system is the system of freedoms, of democracy, of respect and tolerance. Nevertheless, it is the case that the intellectual framework of neo-liberal thinking has always been presented to us in a 'polarized' manner, in the sense that the 'perfect market' is one pole, whereas at the opposite pole lies 'chaos'.⁵ As is to be expected, this polarization between 'perfection' and 'chaos' results in a situation in which those who are not with the market are sunk in penury. In other words, the neo-liberal system radically discounts those who do not identify with it, to the extent of considering them extremely dangerous agents, people who will lead us into chaos, which is to say perdition, total ruination. This means that neo-liberal capitalism, while appearing to be a system of freedoms, in reality tolerates only the freedom of those who do not question the capitalist system. The rest are consigned irreversibly to outer darkness. This in turn means that capitalism, in the same way as Stalinist Communism and Hitlerian Nazism, is a system that tolerates all types of attack except any that poses a serious threat to the system itself. In this sense it is also a system without freedom, since it allows freedom only within the limits set by the system itself and in accordance with the interests of the system itself.

The failure of twentieth-century utopias, however, includes something more significant. The most serious problem presented by the three great utopias mentioned is that they have proved incapable of producing a critique of existing reality. The worst aspect of all is that, in view of the failures and frustrations they have heaped upon us, they have also been incapable of putting forward a proposal for what ought to exist. On the contrary, first Stalinist Communism, then Hitler's Nazism, and finally free-market capitalism, precisely because they have been incapable of producing a critique of what they have brought us, have also been unable to suggest what might be able to rescue us from this disordered and 'runaway' world.⁶ This is why the twentieth century has been the century of the crisis of utopian thought, with this crisis forming one of the signs indicative of so-called postmodernity.⁷ The great words no longer apply: for the vast majority of people neither great projects nor sublime ideals any longer make sense. And we have to resign ourselves to the 'feeble thinking' that produces, among other things, the conviction that our life in human history has no liberating meaning, in accordance with the familiar ideas of Vattimo and Lyotard.⁸ At the end of the twentieth century and start of the twenty-first, we have reached rock-bottom on the dark road of loss of hope and, for many, the tragedy of despair. This is how things stand, I believe, at the present time, the only exception being alternative movements, which fortunately have not died and represent what hope is left to us.

II. Utopia and hope

A society in which utopias cannot be born and nourished is one in which the hope of history has been reduced to the limited aspiration of clinging on to what one has. Briefly, a society without utopias is a society without hope. And this makes it a society in which some, the privileged, focus their aspirations on holding on to what they have, while the great majority, those excluded and marginalized, cannot get beyond the despairing desire for survival, the lowest expression of the instinct for preservation.

This verdict on what is happening in our globalized society is undoubtedly harsh, perhaps too negative, certainly pessimistic. But, however unpleasant the outcome, we have to put things in these terms and face the facts of what is happening. Utopias have been the driving force of history. If there have been changes in the course of human history and if people have nourished hopes, this has been due to the existence of influential individuals or groups who did not conform to what they had and who, as a result, wanted society and people's lives to be different and certainly better, more worthy, more secure and more hope-filled. Today this is generally difficult, not to say virtually impossible, at least for the moment and in the short term. Why?

At the time when, more than forty years ago, Leszek Kolakowski wrote 'Mankind with no Alternative',[9] there were those who thought that there was no alternative, either for the Stalinist economy or within the capitalist means of production themselves. Capitalism, after all, is the most efficient system, in that it produces the highest rates of economic growth seen up till now. And, there is no doubt, the economic growth produced over the past four decades has proved those who thought in this way in the 1960s right. From this two consequences have been drawn: 1. the market economy is the only economy to which there is no alternative; 2. the effectiveness of the market has been elevated to the supreme criterion of values.[10] This means that what is most effective for the market has finally come to be considered what is best for human beings. As a result, economic efficacy has, for many people, become the determining principle of ethical behaviour. In fact, many businessmen and economists in the wealthy countries have become convinced that the destitution of the poor countries can be explained by the fact that the politicians and businessmen of these poor countries are corrupt. In other words, there is bad ethical behaviour where the market economy works badly, while the good are those who prosper economically. The criterion of economic efficacy has been elevated, in the view of the 'satisfied', into a criterion of morality.

There is no need for much brainstorming to understand that, to the extent that this outcome reflects something that is really going on, so we can state that we are living in a disordered culture and in a highly dangerous situation. Among other reasons, this is because all this has led to our being satisfied by a society in which economic development, meaning the production of private goods, has turned out to be more important and more effective than social development, in the sense of production of common goods. In this way we have organized a society in which the satisfied (who are the minority) live more satisfied every day and without wishing anything to change, while the unsatisfied (who are the great majority) live resigned to bare survival and without being able to aspire to changes that might substantially modify their expectations for the future.

How can one explain that all this is happening without the huge majority of unsatisfied people rebelling against the minority of those who live best? Or, more directly, what explanation is there for the fact that, with things as they are, utopias achievable in the short and medium term are not appearing? In the last three years, many people have read the book by the young and brilliant writer Naomi Klein, *No Logo: Taking Aim at the Brand*. The hypothesis she proposes is that 'as the secrets that lie behind the world network of (commercial) brands become known by an increasing number of persons, their exasperation will provoke the great political upheaval of the future, which will consist in a vast wave of outright rejection of transnational corporations and especially those whose brands are most widely known'.[11] That is, the author's view is that alternatives are not sought because people do not really know what is happening. In other words, what is at stake is an information problem. I would agree with this. But is this the only explanation for the apathy of some and the resignation of others? Is it simply ignorance that lies behind the absence of utopia?

There is one fact that is widely borne out by experience: the offer of immediate satisfaction provided by the neo–liberal market has proved to be much stronger and more compelling, for the generality of mortals, than the offers made by social and religious movements.[12] This explains the fact that there are many people who know the manipulations of the market by heart, who do not agree with such abominations, and who nevertheless feel satisfied by this model of the economy and society and do not wish things to change. Because, for the ordinary run of people, satisfaction of needs is more decisive than coherence of ideas. Undoubtedly, this speaks for itself where human beings are concerned. Of course, from the point of view of theoretical reflection, I cannot believe it to be right. But experience shows us that this is what most people do in their daily lives. Because the earliest and strongest things we feel, when we come into the world, are needs. Then, as time goes on, we begin to learn to have ideas. This is why needs are usually more compelling than ideas. And it is also the reason for the frequent dissociation that occurs between what we think and what we do. Of course, in saying these things I am not talking of the lives of heroes. But the fact is that, in this world, heroes are in a tiny minority.

III. How to regain utopia?

For more than fifty years experience has been teaching us that there is a deep connection between a conservative mentality on the one hand, a capitalist mentality on the other, and, as a third component, an anti–utopian mentality. One author who has best expressed this connection has been David Stockman, in his book *The Triumph of Politics* (1986). These three interconnecting mentalities combine to form the foundations of the dominant thinking of the period. This is a form of thinking that Stockman himself summed up perfectly when he described one of his most eloquent experiences: '. . . with what trepidation I found myself in the hall of the UN building, that bastion of the defenders of *détente*, of communists and of left–wing heretics. I trembled at the thought of God's wrath at my presence in this marketplace of wickedness . . .'[13]

It is true that this form of thinking is extreme, because it is pitched at the limit of reality, not to say beyond any form of reality one can verify. But the seriousness of the matter lies in the fact that it is shared by not a few of the magnates of world capital and the makers of the most violent politics of the historical moment at which we are living. Furthermore – and this is decisive – *this* form of thinking is nourished, to a large extent, by religion. Which is understandable. Such aggressive and brutal thinking needs due 'legitimation' in order to justify itself to public opinion. But such 'legitimation' can be provided only by religion. Hence the decisive involvement of religions at this moment in global violence, including terrorist violence. Because of this, and for other reasons, the great religious institutions are no longer inspirers of utopias but forces that powerfully help to underpin the established system.

This means two things: 1. While religions continue to be bound up in the (economic and political) system, it will not be possible to regain utopia. 2. Religions will go on being an integral part of the system and will go on 'legitimizing' this violent and even criminal system for as long as the system goes on providing economic, legal and political means to enable religions to maintain their personnel, their churches, their worship, and, of course, to keep fomenting a private and public morality that supports violence, is silent in the face of attacks on human rights, and justifies such behaviour on the pretext of its condemnations of sex and abortion and its defence of religious education, which each confession pursues in order to catechize its followers.

Translated by Paul Burns

Notes

1. M. Horkheimer, 'La utopía', in A. Neusüss (ed.), *Utopía*, Barcelona 1971, p. 97.
2. F. Hinkelammert, *Crítica de la razón utópica*, Bilbao 2002, p. 10.
3. Ibid., p. 261. (Mrs Thatcher's repeated assertion that 'There is no alternative' earned her the nickname TINA for a while. -Trans.)
4. K. Popper, 'Utopía y violencia', in Neusüss, *Utopia* (n.1), p. 133.
5. Hinkelammert, *Crítica* (n.2), p. 135.
6. Anthony Giddens, *Runaway World: The Effects of Globalization on our Lives*, London 1999.
7. J. A. Pérez Tapias, *Filosofía y crítica de la cultura*, Madrid 1995, p. 102.
8. Ibid., pp. 114–17.
9. L. Kolakowski, *Der Mensch ohne Alternative*, Munich 1960.
10. Hinkelammert, *Crítica* (n.2), pp. 260–1.
11. Naomi Klein, *No Logo. Taking Aim at the Brand*, Toronto 2000.
12. Cf. Susan George, *The Lugano Report: On Preserving Capitalism in the Twenty-first Century*, London 1999, new edition 2003.
13. *Der Spiegel* 17, 1986, p. 177.

Imaging God and 'A Different World'

SALLIE MCFAGUE

*'We wake, if we wake at all, to mystery, rumours of death, beauty, violence . . .
'Seem like we're just set down here,' a woman said to me recently, 'and don't
nobody know why.' . . . Some unwonted, taught pride diverts us from our original
intent, which is to explore the neighbourhood, view the landscape, to discover
where it is that we have been so startlingly set down, even if we can't learn why'.*[1]

Introduction

When we wake up to the mystery that surrounds us, its beauty and its
violence, we ask, 'Why are we here?' 'Seem like we're just set down here . . .
and don't nobody know why.' Indeed. Most religions are about suggesting
answers to that question, which is a fiendishly difficult one. A somewhat
easier, more immediate question is the other one, 'Where are we?' As Annie
Dillard suggests, 'our original intent', as witnessed by a child's interest in
and wonder at all things, is 'to explore the neighbourhood . . . to discover
where it is that we have been so startlingly set down, even if we can't learn
why.'

How do images of God and the world change our perception of what
questions we ask about our world and our behaviour in it? Is another world
possible if we stay with the traditional view of the God–world relationship?
Can we explore the possibilities of our neighbourhood – our world – if our
major images of God do not support such an interest? If a different world is
to be possible, then, one task is to think differently about its relation to God.

How distant, how close, are God and the world? Is God only transcendent
over the world or also immanent in it? Is the relationship between God and
the world more like that between a potter and a bowl or a mother and a child?
Are we only externally related to God or are we internally related? Is the
world more like another 'subject' to God or more like an 'object'? Is God
'spirit' while the world is only 'matter'? Does God have all power over
creation or are human beings also responsible for creation? Are we puppets
or partners? These and many more questions dealing with the nature of the

relationship between God and the world lie at the heart of how we perceive and act in the world.

I. The traditional creation myth

The First Vatican Council (1890) expresses the God-world relationship that, with some variations, is a common one in major creeds of various Christian churches since the Reformation and lies behind the traditional creation/providence story.

> The Holy, Catholic, Apostolic, Roman Church believes and confesses that there is one true and living God, Creator and Lord of Heaven and earth, almighty, eternal, immense, incomprehensible, infinite in intelligence, in will, and in all perfection, who, as being one, sole, absolutely simple and immutable spiritual substance, is to be declared really and essentially distinct from the world, of supreme beatitude in and from himself, and ineffably exalted above all things beside himself which exist or are conceivable.[2]

Given this view of the God-world relationship – one of total distance and difference – the story of creation and providence follows. That story, in its simplest form, claims that an absolute, all-powerful, transcendent God created the world (universe) from nothing for entirely gratuitous reasons. God did not need creation nor is God internally related to it: it was created solely for God's glory. Unfortunately, creation 'fell' through the pride of one of its creatures – human beings – making it necessary for God to initiate a reversal of creation's downfall through Jesus Christ, who atones for the sins of all human beings. In this story creation and providence are part of one coherent, historical, all-inclusive drama in which God is in charge from beginning to end, creating all things and saving them through the atoning blood of his own Son.

This mythic story focuses on God's actions – God is the protagonist of the world drama –and its purpose is to answer why, not where questions. The story speaks to our concerns about why the world was made, who is in charge of it, why it is no longer harmonious, and how it is made 'right' again. This story does not speak to our interest in the world or how we should act towards our neighbours. Human beings are, in fact, minor players in the classic Christian story of creation and providence. Moreover, the action does not occur in our physical neighbourhoods, the actual spaces and places we

inhabit, but over our heads, as it were, in the vast panoramic historical sweep
of time, with its beginning (creation), middle (redemption) and end (eschatology). In each of these events God is totally in charge; we, at most, like good
children are grateful to our all-mighty, all-loving Father and try to follow his
will. Even when sin and evil divert the drama from its triumphant course
(and cause us to lose faith and hope), the Lord of history will prevail, the
King will be victorious.

What is left out of this story of creation is creation itself, that is, 'the
neighbourhood', the lowly, concrete, particular – and fascinating, wonderful – details of physical reality. In fact, the story does not seem to be about
creation, but about a God whose 'spiritual substance . . . is to be declared
really and essentially distinct from the world'. This God does not inhabit
creation; in fact, the assumption behind this creation story is that spirit and
matter are entirely distinct and in a dualistic, hierarchical relationship. God
– and all things spiritual, heavenly, and eternal — is perfect and exalted
above all things material, earthly and mortal, the latter being entirely
different from the former and inferior to it. It is difficult to overstate the
importance of this assumption –the dualistic, hierarchical relationship of
God and the world — for it not only encourages an understanding of salvation as the escape of individuals to the spiritual world, but also justifies lack
of attention to the flourishing of this world. If God is spirit and creation is
matter, then God does not occupy the earth and we need not attend to it
either. But what if spirit and matter were not entirely different? What if all
life – God's and ours, as well as that of all others on earth – was seen to be on
a continuum, more like a circle or a recycle symbol than like a dualistic
hierarchy? What if spirit and matter were intrinsically related, rather than
diametrically opposed? Would not this make a difference in how we thought
of where God is and where we should be? Would it not turn our eyes to the
earth, whether we were searching for God or trying to understand where we
belong?

II. The world as God's body

What if we did not insist on radical dualism between God and the world,
with God being all spirit and the world being all matter or body, but imagined a model with God and the world being both? That is, what if the world
were seen to be God's body which is infused by, empowered by, loved by,
given life by God? What if the world were seen to be 'within' God, not identical with God (as our own bodies are not identical with us, for we can reflect

about them, guide them, direct them, etc.), but very, very intimately connected – like a baby in the womb? Would such a model be a way of expressing profound interrelationship between God and the world, a way that might be closer to an incarnational understanding of the God–world relationship than the other models we have considered?

Augustine helps us along the way with his wonderful sense of our ontological intimacy with God as expressed in this passage from his *Confessions*:[3]

> Since I do indeed exist and yet would not exist unless you were in me, why do I ask you to come to me? . . . Therefore, my God, I would not exist at all, unless you were in me; or rather, I would not exist unless I were in you 'from whom and by whom and in whom all things exist' . . . To what place do I call to you to come, since I am in you? Or from what place are you to come to me? Where can I go beyond the bounds of heaven and earth that my God may come to, for he has said: 'I fill heaven and earth?'

If God is always incarnate, then Christians should attend to the model of the world as God's body. For Christians, God did not become human on a whim; rather, it is God's nature to be embodied, to be the One in whom we live and move and have our being. In Christianity, the God–world relationship is understood in light of the incarnation; hence, creation is 'like' the incarnation. Jesus Christ is the lens, the model, through whom Christians interpret God, world and themselves. The doctrine of creation for Christians, then, is not different in kind from the doctrine of the incarnation: in both God is the source of all existence, the One in whom we are born and re-born. In this view, the world is not just matter while God is spirit; rather, there is a continuity (though not an identity) between God and the world. The world is flesh of God's 'flesh'; the God who took our flesh in one person, Jesus of Nazareth, has always done so. God is incarnate, not secondarily but primarily. Therefore, an appropriate Christian model for understanding creation is the world as God's body. This is not a description of creation (there are no descriptions); neither is it necessarily the only model; it is, however, one model that is commensurate with the central Christian affirmation that God is with us in the flesh in Jesus Christ and it is a model that is particularly appropriate for interpreting the Christian doctrine of creation in our time. Its merits and limitations should be considered in relation to other major models of the God–world relationship: God as clockmaker winding up the machine, as king of the realm, as father with wayward children, as personal agent acting in the world, and so forth.

An incarnational understanding of creation says that nothing is too lowly, too physical, too mean a labour if it helps some creature to flourish. We find God in caring for the garden. Hence, this understanding of creation asks us to find out about the neighborhood so we can take care of it. It suggests that human beings are not the only creatures that matter; however, we are special. We are the caretakers, the ones who can help the garden flourish, help the body of God to be well fed and healthy – or we can destroy it. We know the difference between good and evil: the unique feature of human beings as well as our greatest burden is that we know that we know. We not only know how to do many things (all animals know this), but we know that we can do many things, and that some of these things are good and some bad for God's creation, God's body, our planetary garden.

Let us look more carefully at a couple of implications of this model. The implications of the model of the world as God's body are, first, that we must know our world and where we fit into it; second, that we must acknowledge God as the only source of all life, love, truth and goodness.

III. Knowing the body, tending the garden

In our model, the body of God is the entire universe; it is all matter in its myriad, fantastic, ancient and modern forms, from quarks to galaxies. More specifically, the body of God needing our attention is planet earth, a tiny piece of divine embodiment that is our home and garden. In order to care for this garden, we need to know about it; in order to help all creatures who constitute this body flourish, we need to understand how we humans fit into this body.

All understandings of creation and providence rest on assumptions about what the world is like and where human beings belong in it. First-century Mediterranean, medieval and eighteenth-century views of the world and the place of humans differ; the twenty-first century view does as well. In our evolutionary, ecological view of reality, everything is interrelated and inter-dependent. 'Ecological unity' is both radically individualistic and radically relational. In an organism or body, the whole flourishes only when all the different parts function well; in fact, the 'whole' is nothing but each and every individual part doing its particular thing successfully. Nothing is more unified than a well-functioning body but, also, nothing relies more on complex, diverse individuality.

Hence, the neighbourhood that we have been set down in is one that we must learn to care for in all its diverse parts and needs. We must become 'ecologically literate', understanding its most basic law: that there is no way the whole can flourish unless all parts are cared for. This means that distributive justice is the key to sustainability; or, to phrase it differently, our garden home, the body of God, will be healthy in the long term only if all parts of it are cared for appropriately. Before all else, the community, our planet, must survive (sustainability), and it can do so only if all members have access to basic necessities (distributive justice). We need to learn 'home economics', the basic rules of how our garden home can prosper – and what will destroy it. Most simply, these house rules are: take only your share; clean up after yourself; and keep the house in good repair for others.

We must do so because, as the self-reflective part of God's body – the part that knows that we know – we have become partners with God in maintaining the health of creation. We are no longer the peak of creation, the one above all the others and for whom the others were made; rather, we are at one and the same time the neediest of all creatures and the most powerful. We cannot exist beyond a few minutes without air, a few days without water, or a few weeks without the plants, but we are also, given our population and high-energy lifestyle, the one species that can undermine the planet's well-being, as global warming, the decline of biodiversity and the increasing gap between the rich and the poor are illustrating. In a strange paradox, we who have unprecedented power over the planet are at the same time at its mercy: if it does not thrive, neither can we.

As is evident, this first implication of creation modelled as God's body supports and underscores a radically ecological view of the world. It is entirely opposed to the cult of individualism endorsed by modern religion, government and economics, all of which claim that human beings are basically separate, isolated individuals who enter into relationships when they wish. This is the view of human beings that underlies both New Age and born-again Christianity, as well as market capitalism and American democracy ('life, liberty, and the pursuit of happiness'). Perhaps the most important implication of creation as God's body is the new anthropology it demands: we are – basically, intrinsically, and always – interrelational, interdependent beings who live in total dependence on the others who compose the body, while at the same time being responsible for the well-being of one tiny part of the body, planet earth.

IV. God as Source of Life and Love

A second implication of the model of creation as God's body is that it radi-calizes both God's transcendence and God's immanence. This model has been criticized by some as pantheistic, as identifying God and the world. I do not believe that it is. If God is to the universe as each of us is to our bodies, then God and the world are not identical. They are, however, intimate, close and internally related in ways that can make Christianity uncomfortable when it forgets its incarnationalism. But we Christians should not shy away from a model that radically underscores both divine transcendence and divine immanence. How does it do so?

In the world as God's body, God is the source, the centre, the spring, the spirit of all that lives and loves, all that is beautiful and true. When we say 'God', that is what we mean: we mean the power and source of all reality. We are not the source of our own being; hence, we acknowledge the radical dependence of all that is on God. This is true transcendence: being the source of everything that is. Our universe, the body of God, is the reflection of God's being, God's glory; it is the sacrament of God's presence with us. The most radically transcendent understanding of God is, then, at the same time the most radically immanent understanding. Because God is always incarnational, always embodied, we can see God's transcendence immanen-tally. Meeting God is not a momentary 'spiritual' affair; rather, God is the ether, the reality, the body, the garden in which we live. God is never absent; God is reality (being); everything that has being derives it from God (we are born of God and re-born by God). The entire cosmos is born of God, as is each and every creature. We depend on this source of life and renewable absolutely. To realize this is an overwhelming experience of God's transcen-dence; it calls forth awe and immense gratitude. Yet, at the same time, as Augustine puts it, God is closer to us than we are to ourselves. Where can we go where God is not, since God fills heaven and earth? 'I would not exist if I were not in you.' The God whom we meet through the earth is not only the source of my being, but of all being. We see glimmers of God in creation (God's body) and we see the same God more clearly in Jesus Christ, the major model of God for Christians.

The second implication of our model, then, is that is allows us to meet God in the garden, on the earth, at home. We do not have to go elsewhere or wait until we die or even be 'religious'. We meet God in the nitty-gritty of our regular lives, for God is always present in every here and now. This second implication underscores the first: since God is here in our world, then surely it is indeed our neighbourhood, our planet and its creatures that we should be caring for. What other vocation could we have but to care for God's body?

V. Creation or redemption Christianity?

The model of the world as God's body suggests a creation-orientated Christianity in contrast to the tradition's heavy emphasis on redemption. In the end, there are many similarities between the two perspectives, for on each God is both creator and saviour. However, the greatest difference between them is 'where we are at home'. In creation Christianity we are at home here on the earth, an earth that exists within God. We may not know why we have been placed here, but we know where we are: we live within God. We live within God before we are born, during our time on earth, and after we die. We are always in the same place – within God.

In the other version of the Christian story, we are not at home on the earth. To be sure, God came to earth at one point, in the incarnation of the redeemer Jesus Christ, but otherwise God is only externally related to the world. In both stories we belong to God, but in the redemption-orientated one we can only find God in and through Jesus Christ and the community founded by him. We are 'at home' in the church, the body of Christ, but not in the world (which is not seen as the body of God). Our final home, where we really belong, is in another time and another place: we reach this world of eternal life through accepting Christ's reconciling death for our sins. Neither God nor we are at home on the earth; it is not where God is or where we (properly) belong.

But in the model of the world as God's body, there is only one world, our earth, which we inhabit and of which God is the source, spring and power. God is primarily and always incarnated, and creation is the witness of that continuous presence with us. In Jesus of Nazareth, Christians believe that God's embodied presence reaches its culmination; the implicit becomes explicit; the shadows of divine love and goodness, truth and beauty, move into the light. We see the revelation of God in the face of Jesus Christ. In Jesus' ministry of feeding the hungry, healing the sick and siding with the poor and oppressed – actions which countered conventional mores and led to his death – we see concretely what living rightly in God's body means. In the story of Jesus we are brought face to face, as it were, with God's presence, a presence that we have always lived in and at times acknowledged. In this story we learn two things about where we are: we are in God and we are called to live as disciples of Jesus. We live within God; hence, we can relax and enjoy, for we are at home and there is no other place we want to be. We live also (and at the same time) on the earth; hence, we can get busy caring for our garden home. Moreover, the story of Jesus provides us with a vision of how we should care for this home in the kingdom of God, the eucharistic banquet, to which all are invited to share the feast. The story of ecological economics – home economics for planet earth – provides us with a way to work toward that vision: through sharing resources with all creatures so earth may prosper (distributive justice for sustainability).

I close with yet another reminder that all models are partial and inadequate. No one model is adequate, for each allows us to see some aspects of the God-world relationship, but shuts out others. The model of the world as God's body is meant as a corrective to the tradition, not as a substitute for it. It is offered as one model that is commensurate with Christianity's central incarnational belief and, for our time, helpful for the flourishing of all God's creatures. The final word, however, on this model and on all models is one of caution: 'Be careful how you interpret the world; it is like that.'[4]

Notes

A longer version of this article was originally published as 'Is God in Charge? Creation and Providence', in William C.Placher (ed.), *Essentials of Christian Theology*, Louisville, KY 2003, pp. 93–116.

1. Annie Dillard, *Pilgrim at Tinker Creek*, New York 1977, pp. 2, 12.
2. *The Decrees of the Vatican Council*, ed. Vincent McNabb, London 1907.
3. Augustine, *Confessions*, I, 2.
4. Erich Heller, *The Disinherited Mind*, New York 1961, p. 211.

II. A Different World in the Making – A Different Form of Religion

The Shape of God to Come and the Future of Humanity

MUSIMBI KANYORO

'I am not a statistic, I am a woman living with HIV/AIDS. I am a spiritual being having a human experience.' [1]

Brigitte died on 23 February 2003, hardly a year after she spoke those words. Memories of Brigitte bring tears to my eyes. Brigitte also spoke at the Social Forum in Porto Allegro and many other places. Her mission was to dare to confront the stigma that is associated with HIV and AIDS. She addressed the injustices and illness, drawing attention to the fact that the church was assuming that those who live with HIV had sinned. This mother and French teacher had also been a faithful wife. Brigitte, a Catholic by faith, became an activist after testing HIV positive in 1992. She used to say that faith and prayer were about the search for a God of justice.

My former professor in undergraduate studies often used to quote Karl Barth as having once said, ' . . . to clasp hands in prayer is the beginning of an uprising against the disorder of the world'.[2] The story of the persistent woman in Luke 18.1–8 is one of the Bible stories that illustrates the mission of Brigitte and other people of faith who feel motivated to take action on matters of social justice. This story has been used to illustrate Jesus' teaching about persistent prayer to his disciples. But when one reads the story through, one is struck by the fact that persistent prayer is a right-based search for God who grants justice. The story illustrates very clearly that many times justice is denied, and those who have been denied justice have a right to demand it. Justice does not become obsolete in time. The way to correct injustice is to provide justice. Persistence in the search for justice is rooted in the belief that a different world is possible. Our longings for peace and justice, health and wholeness, are foremost spiritual longings. Women of the Bible, women of the church, women of the world like Brigitte inspire me to believe that a different world is possible. My theology, social analysis and Christian living are currently rooted in daily working with women and it is their story of hope for a different world that I want to tell.

I. Spirituality[3] rather than religion

Suppose we were able to identify which attributes should comprise a God to respond to the needs of our world today, for instance peace, love, globalization, social justice, gender equality, sustainable development, security and hope. Where would our search take us? I contend that the search would send us to examine inside our beliefs rather than in our religions. The search for God is basically a search for our spirituality. Spirituality is what permits us to make sense out of life.

I have told the story of the late Brigitte at length to illustrate two points. First, Christian women's participation in social movements has a basis in the church's spirituality, but it is nurtured in the context of movements of people with similar hopes for a better world. The church is hospitable when people feel that the church is a safe place for them in times of need and that the church creates an outreach for them to respond to the needs of the world. Participation helps people to realize that they are not consumers of church theology and doctrines but mutually accountable persons who bear witness to what the church should be. The issues at stake are not just traditional lay and ordained persons or historical debates about the roles of men and women. Today, the driving forces in faith or specifically church debates include the participation of people living with HIV/AIDS, people with different sexual orientation, people with disabilities, migrants, lower income people, indigenous people or people of other faiths or no faith. The search for community is the essence of people's engagement in social advocacy.[4] Social activism is the sum total of the 'spiritual hopes'[5] of various people who engage together or engage each other with the conviction that their actions will make a difference for the common good.

Secondly, although the term 'spirituality' is in vogue, my objective is not to be politically correct but rather to affirm the practices of everyday resistance that I see in people who do not deny God, but rather express their understanding of God differently. People who no longer find meaning in organized religion are willing to explore their spirituality elsewhere. Such people are hungry for a bigger vision of God. Within the past three decades, the peoples of the world have found for themselves new ways of walking and working together across borders in order to respond to human needs. As a result of knowledge and expanded consciousness, people are discarding yesterday's limited exclusiveness and seeking for answers together. Social movements have become central to the search for truth and the search for God is implicit in that.

Christian people who participate in social movements are 'church'. They are 'a community of faith and struggle working to anticipate God's new creation by becoming partners with those who are at the margins of church and society'.[6] Many women of faith refuse the poverty-stricken diet that religions give them. They long to belong to something which includes their concerns, energizes and nourishes them: prayer groups, social justice groups, international groups, artists groups, music groups, ecumenical groups, etc.

Women activists believe in a God who is not aloof from human affairs, but whose reality is grounded in the daily struggles of a people in the quest for justice. The presence of this God is imminent in their agonized cries, which are sometimes very loud and other times very silent. The lives and stories of women convince me that a different world is possible. Women have broken the silence on their oppression and violence; they have accessed education that was denied to them, and they continue to struggle for better access to health care, economic stability, environmental security and human rights for themselves and their communities and families. Women have created shifts in societal attitudes to females, claimed their space in leadership and decision-making, and through their determination have changed the very nature of human society, including religious dogma. Women have accomplished this critical agenda by using a variety of creative methods, organizing for solidarity and mutual support, all in the belief that it is possible to make a difference. Women have done this with limited resources, while continuing to work as mothers, grandmothers, aunts, daughters, career women, public servants, educators, etc. Women have spent the last several decades building trust as a base for the women's movement often under difficult and challenging conditions. Women have been at the margins of the church and society for so long that they have learnt to be 'in the round'. Women in different contexts and locations are demonstrating how faith informs struggles for justice and how struggles for justice inform faith.

Christian women activists spend a great deal of time exploring the question 'How can men and women resolve what keeps us in opposing camps so that we can more fully respond the Bible's call to serve both God and neighbour and to love one another as God loves us?' It is not an easy question, because it evokes more than emotion. The interpretations of the very scriptures that are supposed to serve as the road map to the affirming common humanity of men and women often become a stumbling block to our lives together. Women's actions are about falling into passion with principles that lead us to compassion. Principles are not substitutes for passion. Principles don't move us as passions do, but principles can guide our passions and groom them into compassions. Such principles help us to implement justice, fairness and to be consistent so that we do not become ambiguous in the way that we act.

II. The ecumenical movement rather than the church

The ecumenism found in feminist theologies, liberation theologies and the social actions of churches together has empowered women to move beyond feelings of helplessness in their church's interpretation of women's roles and functions. The ecumenical movement is for many women a place of hospitality where their experienced vulnerability meets divine mercy. It is the place to celebrate and to share experiences as well as to confess our failures. Here women have had a chance to do theology together and to use the biblical and theological resources produced by feminist academic theologians. It is quite remarkable that the church has not embraced the textual interpretations of feminist theology. It is doubly amazing that even though women have been part of the church from the very beginning, the dogmas of the church still argue that women do not belong to the inner circle of those who have to carry the church into the future. Not only are they ignored as persons; their needs, which define their humanity, are not visible in the teaching and even healing role of the church. Women often lament a lack of spiritual recognition of such important rites of passage in their lives such as the birthing of a baby, bleeding, menstruation, menopause, pregnancy, abortion/miscarriage, care-giving and self-affirmation. Efforts to find and reclaim resources for women's spirituality have been made by women belonging to many organized sets of religion such Islam, Buddhism, Christianity Judaism, Native American beliefs and Indigenous African Religions.[7] It is no wonder that the open hospitality of secular social forums is a place where those in the margins find room to be heard. The social forum is not a space to agree on ideologies, but rather to create synergies on particular issues. It is a space for cementing the partnerships for common good.

III. Trust rather than rules

The women's movement is the largest organized people's movement in the world. Women have spent a lifetime building trust as a base for the women's movement, often under difficult and challenging conditions. Trust is essential for social well-being. Stories are not shared or told except in a context of mutual trust. Without trusting the good-will of others, we retreat into rules and regulations and the punishments that follow for those who break the rules. Women in their search for affirmation have often underlined the principles of equality, participation and reciprocity. Words such as partnership, solidarity, sisterhood, friendship, community and togetherness are key to women's conversations. As women talked to one another, we began to discover that our individual experiences of discrimination, triviality, abuse and distortion were not unique to particular women but were indeed universal to women everywhere and in every generation. We found a common ground in hearing the collective story of women's experiences articulated in different contexts and times and yet speaking to the same issues. It is the collective story of womanhood that provided a crucial entry point to women's determination to pursue a space where other possibilities can be experienced. Women's social analysis has both provided the therapy we need in order to be healed from our past and given us the possibility to use our collective knowledge to change our lives, our socialization, our belief systems, and to challenge the teaching we receive from our families, our religions and our societies. Connecting and networking are words that we use to support each other and to build global solidarity.

In the process of listening to each other's stories, we have discovered common themes and trends, but we have also been uncomfortably confronted with differences and sharp distinctions. Our experiences are similar, but they are not homogeneous. We are shaped by very different geographical, historical and social contexts. These in effect determine borders based on economics, race/culture/caste, politics, religion, generation, sexuality, education, health, access to information – and the lists go on. The credibility of women's story is continually challenged by how we acknowledge and manage these differences without being trapped into helplessness, powerlessness, apathy and isolationism.

Other movements, too, value the building of trust as the capital for working together. I belong to the Ecumenical Association of Third World Theologians (EATWOT). We exist because all of us have grown up connected in different ways to the ecumenical movement, and it is from that setting that we can now organize ourselves as Third World theologians. At our assembly in 1992, we adopted as a theme 'Spirituality of the Third World'. As we listened to each other from the Brazilian base communities, Pacific Indigenous People, the Circle of Concerned African Women Theologians, etc., we experienced a similarity through speaking about the tears of our people. We came to terms together with the fact that the cry of the Third World people is a cry for life. It is a cry for the freedom and dignity that constitute life as human. It is a cry for rice and corn, but also a cry for a community that can grow and eat the rice and corn in company of the other. The cry is uttered from the midst of misery, from situations in which the forces of death are rampant and in which children die by thousands from diseases related to malnutrition, yet elsewhere, food is wasted, milk and grain are destroyed and resources are hijacked to provide luxuries and to produce weapons of annihilation.

We cry from the midst of the politics of the powerful who rule our countries with iron hands. Our cry rises from the midst of structures designed for our subjugation, marginalization and extinction, through distorted priorities, skewed agricultural polices, unjust trade arrangements and human and economic manipulations and pressure tactics – all practised and imposed in brutal and subtle ways by neocolonialism and the international imperialism of money built up through the atrocities, cruelties and robberies of the era of military colonialism. We cry from places where people are killed everyday for holding that the poor have a right to live and for believing that children must be given food and justice must be practised. A pastor from Brazil told this story to us.

A mother and her five children broke the law. They built their shack three feet outside the permitted space. Another poor person making a living by working on a bulldozer was brought by the authority to demolish this house. He decided that he could not do so, and therefore chose to go prison than demolish the only shelter of this poor family. While facing his own trial he was asked why he did not obey the orders of the law. His answer was simple. 'I did not know what I would have told my own children.' What shall we tell our children about God and about humanity if we use each other to destroy what God created?

The kind of resistance illustrated above speaks words of hope. It says explicitly that a different world is possible and we can experience it by allowing courage, wisdom and resistance to hold hands and celebrate the power of collective actions. Yet we must always recognize that hope is a fragile quality that is quickly destroyed by any feelings of powerlessness or self-doubt. Social indifference and cultural obligations can bind body, mind and soul in such a way that hope is squeezed out and the result is immediate shrinking. Unless powerlessness is addressed, today's hope will be tomorrow's despair. The success of the social movements can be judged by how they help people take control over their own lives. The capacity for people to manage themselves develops quite unobtrusively when it is accompanied by positive care and affirmation through respectful relationships. Mutual sharing of strength and vulnerabilities creates condition for sustainable partnerships. Encouraging people to renounce lies and embrace truth about them can be difficult and frustrating, but that is the essence of creating networks and organized groups where participants find the safety of being in the companionship of others with similar beliefs and experiences. In these places people become empowered by hearing each other's stories. Most instances of empowerment are not instantaneous. But whether the process is short and immediate or long and tedious, the essence of empowerment entails renunciation of lies and speaking the truth about oneself and the world in which we live. The immediate indicator of empowerment is the move from despair to hope.

IV. Invitation to God's spirituality

Living in line with the mission of Jesus is at the heart of those who do social advocacy in the framework of the church and the Christian faith. According to Jesus (Luke 4.16–19), the spirit of God inspired the creative yet controversial actions he took to give hope to those he met regardless of the consequences. According to Jesus, the concern of the Spirit of God was to speak for the poor, for the victims of cruelty and systematic injustices, for prisoners, the disabled, the sick and those locked out of any meaningful participation in society by bars of ignorance. The concern of the God of Jesus was particularly for people in whom all hope had been crushed – who felt consigned to long days and even longer nights of quiet desperation and despair. According to Jesus, the concern of the Spirit was to motivate people to share the good news with these forgotten ones. The commitment of the Spirit was to motivate people to have a passionate compassion – to be prepared to struggle in solidarity with them for release from all personal, social and political forces that would debilitate them if left and abandoned on their own. The goal of the compassion is to set them free to realize their potential, to be fully human and fully alive, as members of the human community, persons of dignity, persons who can claim the ownership of abundant life.

The essence of being a Christian is to live and act in sympathy with God's Spirit as Jesus did. This implies that we have to be known for keeping the company of beggars, thieves, prostitutes, tax collectors in whatever names and forms that they come to us today. When we take option in favour of the poor we must know that poor people are not a random cross-section of population because poverty does not come randomly. You are more likely to be poor if you are of lower caste, indigenous, black, woman or under eighteen years of age. Poor people lack opportunities to realize their potential. They lack power, influence, voice, and they are extremely vulnerable to sickness, violence and disasters. People who are poor live with a toxic environment, crime, low quality education, and are feared by others. They stand accused of flaunting the values by which 'decent people' live while claiming rights to benefits they have not worked for. The life of the poor is painted as a hot-bed of moral laxity, sexual abuse, loose marital ties and neglect of parental duties. Poor people are often branded as dishonest, lazy, addicted to welfare, capable of fraud, corruption, bribe, vice, drug addiction, alcoholism and substance abuse, criminality, youth hooliganism, theft, mugging, robbery, pick-pocketing, etc.

This makes the realities of poverty less visible to better-off persons who may see these effects as crimes of the poor and advocate for policies victimize them and punish them. The cost of eradicating poverty was once estimated at a mere 1 per cent of global income, that is about 80 billion.[8] In June 2004, the USA congress approved US$87 billion as additional money to be spent on the war in Iraq. It is about time that we stopped worrying about poverty and began to worry about wealth and the harm it is doing to our world. If we do so, we could shape a future which would lay the foundation for the hope that is inbuilt in a UNICEF report which says:

The day will come when nations will be judged not by their military or economic strength, nor by the splendour of their cities and capital cities, but by the well-being of their peoples; by their levels of health, nutrition and education; by their opportunities to earn a fair reward for their labours; by their ability to participate in the decisions that affect their lives; by the respect that is shown for their civil and political liberties; by the provision that is made for those that are vulnerable and disadvantaged; and by the protection that is accorded to the growing minds and bodies of their children.[9]

Notes

1. Brigitte Syamalevwe spoke these words in Addis Ababa, Ethiopia, on 5 August 2002. She was addressing religious leaders, government ministers, diplomats, journalists, invited dignitaries and women theologians and researchers. The occasion was the opening of a conference of African Women Theologians on the theme 'Sex, Stigma and HIV/AIDS– African Women Challenging Religion, Culture and Social Practices'.
2. Micere Mugo, class lecture notes.
3. Deepak Chopra, *How to Know God. The Soul's Journey into the Mystery of Mysteries*, New York 2000.
4. It is always important to be reminded that the Christian life, while intensely personal, is always communal; the privatization of piety is not part of the Christian tradition and it undermines the Christian faith.
5. I use the term 'spiritual hopes' because the determination comes from within and the determination that they will make a difference does not have material object proof.
6. Letty M. Russell, *Church in the Round, Feminist Interpretation of the Church*, Louisville, KY 1993.
7. See Letty Russell and and J. Shannon Clarkson (eds), *Dictionary of Feminist Theologies*, Louisville, KY 1996, pp. 274–7.
8. *Human Development Report 1997*, UNDP.
9. *The Progress of the Nations*, UNICEF Report 2000, p.1.

A New Spirituality for a Religiously Plural World

PERRY SCHMIDT-LEUKEL

There was a time when the majority of Christians did not take any notice of other religions. Even if they knew about their existence, this knowledge did not affect their spirituality. The very few who were concerned about non-Christians usually regarded other religions as more or less dark and hostile forces, as something that should be overcome by Christian mission. Interfaith encounter, if it existed at all, was primarily seen as an opportunity to communicate the Christian gospel. As Karl Barth expressed it only fifty years ago: Christianity 'alone has the commission and the authority to . . . confront the world of religions as the one true religion, . . . to invite and challenge it to abandon its ways and to start on the Christian way'.[1]

I remember quite well a conversation with one of my former theological teachers when I was a postgraduate student. At that time I was writing my thesis on Buddhist-Christian dialogue, and the professor of mission tried to convince me of the superiority of Christianity. As one piece of evidence he claimed that in no other religion could the high ideal of loving one's enemy be found. I contradicted him and told him about the Buddha's parable of the saw, where the Buddha exhorted his disciples that even if someone came with a sharp saw to cut them into pieces bit by bit, they should stay free from any hatred or malevolence and embrace that person with undiminished love and compassion (*Majjhima-Nikâya 21*). The professor was impressed by my objection, but then he responded: 'This makes dialogue with Buddhism even more difficult.' Obviously the only objective of interfaith dialogue that he could think of was to demonstrate to the other the superiority of the Christian gospel.

I must confess that I could understand my professor, for there had been a time when I felt the same. But through my encounter with Buddhism my attitude had changed radically. Today I believe that the time for such a mentality has gone. I am well aware that this mentality is far from being extinct. But I am convinced that it is no longer adequate. Or to be more precise, it never was adequate, but nowadays this has become more apparent than ever before. What we now need to develop is an attitude which permits us to let non-Christians and their religious traditions become a positive part of our own religious consciousness, that is, of our spirituality. The new spirituality for a religiously plural world needs to be an interfaith spirituality. In what follows I would like to sketch some major features of this spirituality by what could be called its seven virtues.

The first virtue is *confidence:* confidence or trust in the basic goodness of the deeper nature or structure of reality; confidence that there is an ultimate reality underlying and transcending, but also permeating, surface reality which suffers from so many obvious limitations and partly horrendous evils. If this confidence is justified, if an ultimate reality really exists, then this gives reason for what John Hick has called 'cosmic optimism'.[2] Being our highest good, ultimate reality is the decisive factor for our understanding of reality in general and for our view of our fellow humans in particular. As it is said by Paul in Acts (17.27): 'God is not far from each one of us; for in him we live and move and exist'. As Paul admits, this has not only been affirmed by Christians. Indeed, what within Christianity is called the 'universal saving will of God' (cf. I Tim. 2.4) has a number of parallels and functional equivalents in other religions. In Islam, the Holy Qur'an (16.36) proclaims: 'For We assuredly sent Amongst every People a messenger (With the Command), "Serve Allah, and eschew Evil" . . .'

In Hinduism we find the deep conviction that God is present in the innermost self of all beings, and that, as Lord Krishna says in the *Bhagavadgîtâ* (9.23): 'Even those who are devotees of other gods, worship them with faith – they also sacrifice to Me alone . . .' In Buddhism there is the widespread doctrine of a universal Buddha-Nature, that is the view that all beings have the potential for realizing enlightenment and ultimate salvation, and in the famous *Lotos-Sûtra* (5.45f.) the supramundane Buddha exclaims: 'As the rays of the sun and moon descend alike on all men, good and bad . . . so the wisdom of the Tathâgata (the Buddha) shines like the sun and the moon, leading all beings without partiality.'

The goodness of ultimate reality is of universal significance, hence we find throughout the religions various expressions of the confidence that the saving presence of the Divine is not confined to one's own religious community. This is also the tenor of biblical passages like Amos 9.7, where we read the powerful message that Israel is not the only elect people, and that

God has liberated other people from their own captivities as he has Israel. A similar confidence is expressed in Jesus' vision of the great eschatological feast, a banquet which will assemble the 'many who shall come from east and west' (Matt. 8.5–11). And there is the deep and bold statement of John's first letter (I John 4.7) that 'everyone who loves is born of God and knows God'. The confidence that the saving presence of divine reality is not confined to one's own faith community leads me to the second virtue of interfaith spirituality, which is

Humility. In this context humility means not to confine the divine reality to our human ways of thinking. God, or the Transcendent, is infinitely greater than all our thoughts, ideas and concepts. For Anselm of Canterbury God was not only that 'than which a greater cannot be conceived'. For being so, God must necessarily be 'greater than everything that can be conceived' (*Proslogion* 15). Thomas Aquinas joins in by saying that 'the divine substance surpasses every form that our intellect reaches' (*Summa contra Gentiles* 14.3). Forgetting God's ineffability would be idolatry, that is, worshipping an idol created by our own concepts, warns Nicholas of Cusa (*De docta ignorantia* I 26,86). The fundamental insight into the necessary inconceivability and ineffability of the divine can be found not only in the writings of all major theologians of the Christian tradition;[3] it has also been frequently expressed in other religious traditions. The Muslim exclamation *Allâhu akbar* does not simply mean 'God is great' but rather and literally 'God is *greater*', greater than everything we could think of. Therefore we should refrain from making any pictures of God, whether with our hands or with our minds. The Eastern religions abound with affirming the limitation of human concepts when it comes to ultimate reality. 'It is not this, not that' (*Brhadâranyaka Upanishad IV*, 5.15), 'there the eyes go not, speech goes not, nor the mind' (*Kena Upanishad* 1.3), say the Hindu Upanishads. And the *Tao Te King* (1.1) begins with the famous words: 'The *Tao* that can be described is not the eternal Tao. The name that can be spoken is not the eternal Name.'

The insight into the ineffable nature of transcendent reality implies that none of the doctrines and teachings of any of the religious communities can exhaust divine reality in its fullness. This should save us from any claims of absoluteness for our own religious tradition.

Transcendent reality is not confined to being transcendent. It is also immanent. Its inconceivability does not prevent it from being present and accessible in the religious experience of humankind. It is apprehended in limited and variegated ways which inevitably reflect our own limitations as finite human beings, but mark at the same time the variety and diversity of humanity. Therefore the third virtue of interfaith spirituality is

Curiosity. Traditionally curiosity was hardly regarded as a virtue, and in particular Augustine saw it more as a vice. I certainly do not mean any forward, insensitive or indecent curiosity, but rather the curiosity of an explorer or scientist. In an interfaith context this designates a genuine interest in what God has meant and still means in the lives of other people; the wish to discover 'the riches which a generous God has distributed among the nations', as the Second Vatican Council stated (*Ad gentes* 11). When Cardinal Ratzinger once was asked by an interviewer, 'How many ways to God are there?', his reply was 'As many as there are human beings'.[4] Curiosity as an interfaith virtue implies taking this seriously. It is the wish to learn more about and from humanity's manifold ways to God, a readiness to enlarge our own spiritual horizon by gaining a better understanding of our neighbours in the other faith-communities, of their experience, their wisdom, their truth. This kind of curiosity will automatically lead to a dialogical attitude, which brings us to the next and central virtue of

Friendship. The curiosity that I have just mentioned will involve reading and studying the scriptures of other religious traditions, learning about their cultural and cultic expressions and sometimes possibly even sharing in other forms of religious practice. But all that we can observe, study and investigate is only expressive of something more profound, but less objectifiable, that is, the faith of real people. We should not forget that the so-called 'religions' are not abstract entities. If a 'religion' is not the religion of real, living persons, it either no longer exists or it never existed at all. All too often we may have an image of other people's religion which is entirely fictitious, because the religion we imagine is not identical with the religion that is lived and experienced by them. We can study many facts about other religious traditions, but what these traditions really mean for those who live in them can, at the end of the day, be understood only through becoming friends with them – good friends! Wilfred Cantwell Smith once remarked that understanding another religion, as for example Buddhism, would mean seeing the world, 'so far as possible, through Buddhist eyes'.[5] Friendship entails a number of good things, one being the effort and ability to understand our friends as they understand themselves. Only when we share their joys and sufferings will we have a chance of understanding how their faith helps them to cope with their sorrow and how it nourishes their hope. This is the kind of under-standing which is crucial for interfaith spirituality and it makes friendship a key virtue.

Friends can be honest with each other. And they have to be honest if they wish to stay true friends. Inter-religious friendship therefore entails the virtue of *honesty* – being honest about the religion of our friend as well as about our own. There is no need to brag and no room for contempt. Let us try simply to be honest and avoid weighing with two measures. For example, let us not compare all the nice ideals in the theory of our own religion with all the horrible failures in the practice of the others. Jesus' parable of the speck in our neighbour's eye and the log in our own eye is highly relevant to interfaith relationships. If there is any need for criticism, it should be uttered cautiously and with much sensitivity. In Christianity there has been the tradition of *correctio fraterna*, the 'admonition among brothers', and I suggest that interfaith criticism, if and when it is necessary, should be carried out in this spirit.

If there is interfaith friendship and honesty, we will not only learn to see the world through the eyes of our friend. We will also begin to see ourselves and our own religion through the eyes of others. I think that it is a clear sign of a maturing interfaith relationship if we as Christians start to perceive ourselves through the eyes of our non-Christian friends.[6] This is certainly a challenging experience, but it has the potential to become a transforming and enriching one. The virtue it requires is

Courage. We need to be courageous in order to expose ourselves and our own religious background to insights from another religious tradition. Seeing oneself through the eyes of the other can help to overcome misunderstand-ings and misperceptions. But it will also call us out of our usual ways and can at times be quite irritating. Let me give just one example. The Jewish theologian Michael Wyschogrod has once pointed out that for all Christians, whether conservative or liberal, the name Jesus and the symbol of the cross evoke uplifting sentiments; for Jews, however, they are 'not a source of comfort but of fear'.[7] What does it mean for us, as Christians, if we become aware that the cherished name and symbol which mean so much to us can and sometimes do have such a contrary meaning for our friends from other faiths? Seeing ourselves and our own religious traditions through the eyes of others will inevitably make us aware of a number of all too human shortcomings and limitations and help us to gain a far more realistic self-understanding.

Inter-religious dialogue, if it is genuine and serious, therefore leads to an 'intra-religious dialogue'.[8] Intra-religious dialogue starts when we allow ourselves to be challenged by the insights coming from our friends and from their religious backgrounds. Do their insights require a change in my thinking, my feeling, my believing? Courage implies the readiness to draw any spiritual consequences which naturally result from an honest exposure to a religious tradition other than one's own. It is a courage for change. A number of people who seriously entered into interfaith dialogue, interfaith encounter, interfaith friendship have felt that after many years of such an exposure they became significantly transformed – some even to the degree of now feeling a kind of 'double' or 'multiple belonging'.[9] That is, in their own personal spirituality they are no longer nourished by one religious tradition alone. No doubt this is a substantial transformation, but in the sense of an existentially or spiritually crucial enrichment leaving those who made the experience with a sense of deep gratitude.

Gratitude is the last in my list of seven virtues of interfaith spirituality. Gratitude for the other, gratitude for what we have in common as well as for our differences. I remember reading a review in which the reviewer blamed a certain author for being 'unsure of whether the good thing about the world faiths is that we are all the same or whether it is that we are all different'.[10] What a wrong alternative! Let us rejoice in both our unity and our diversity. Let us be grateful for both.

If gratitude is deep and profound it implies what German mystics have called *Gelassenheit*. The term covers meanings like calmness, equanimity, and letting go or not being attached. Detachment is of course a major spiritual feature of the Eastern religions, while the religions of the West have primarily emphasized loving involvement. Detachment and involvement are different, but not antagonistic. A closer look into the spiritual traditions of the East and the West shows that both are not only compatible but complementary. Without loving involvement detachment will pervert into unconcerned self-indulgence; without detachment loving involvement will degenerate into spiritless activism or even ideological fanaticism. Interfaith spirituality may help us – not only 'us Christians' but all of us – to learn better and understand how both can be kept together, for our own sake and the sake of the world.

Notes

1. Karl Barth, *Church Dogmatics* I/2, §17 no.3, Edinburgh 1975, p. 357.
2. Cf. John Hick, *An Interpretation of Religion. Human Responses to the Transcendent*, Houndmill 1989, pp. 56–69; id., *The Fifth Dimension. An Exploration of the Spiritual Realm*, Oxford 1999, pp. 47–73.
3. It is therefore all the more suprising and deploring that it has been recently renounced by *Dominus Iesus* no. 6 in order to safeguard the superiority claims of the present magisterium of the Roman Catholic Church.
4. Josef Ratzinger, *Salz der Erde. Christentum und katholische Kirche an der Jahrtausendwende. Ein Gespräch mt Peter Seewald*, Stuttgart 1996, p. 35.
5. Cf. Wilfred Cantwell Smith, *Towards a World Theology. Faith and the Comparative History of Religion*. Maryknoll, NY 1989, p. 82.
6. See for example: Paul Griffith (ed.), *Christianity Through Non-Christian Eyes*, Maryknoll, NY 1990; Lloyd Ridgeon (ed.), *Islamic Interpretations of Christianity*, Richmond, VA 2001; Perry Schmidt-Leukel (ed.), *Buddhist Perceptions of Jesus*, St Ottilien 2001.
7. Michael Wyschogrod, 'A Jewish Postscript', in S. Davis (ed.), *Encountering Jesus. A Debate on Christology*, Atlanta, GA 1988, pp. 179–87: p. 179.
8. Cf. Raimundo Panikkar, *The Intrareligious Dialogue*, New York 1978.
9. Cf. Catherine Cornille (ed.), *Many Mansions? Multiple Belonging and Christian Identity*, Maryknoll, NY 2002; Harold Kasimow, John P. Keenan and Linda Klepinger Keenan (eds), *Beside Still Waters. Jews, Christians, and the Way of the Buddha*, Boston 2003; Peter Phan, 'Multiple Religious Belonging: Opportunities and Challenges for Theology and Church', *Theological Studies* 64, 2003, pp.495–519. While multiple religious belonging is a relatively new phenomenon in the Western religious traditions, it is of course far more familiar in the East. Hence it is not surprising that the issue is particularly raised in dialogue with Eastern religions. See for example John Berthrong, *All Under Heaven. Transforming Paradigms in Confucian-Christian Dialogue*, New York 1994, pp. 65–87.
10. Kelvin Holdsworth, 'Songs designed to make you think', *The Scottish Episcopalian*, June 2003, no. 221, p. 6.

The God of Jesus and the Possibilities of History

CLAUDE GEFFRÉ OP

Above all since the disastrous war waged by the Americans against Iraq, terrorism has remained a permanent threat to the whole of global civilization. It has its source in the fanaticism of a certain number of extremist Muslims. But it also feeds on the immense frustration of people who are the victims of a globalization which not only maintains the structural injustice of the contemporary world but increases it. In that case the sign of the time which brings hope to today's world is the collective awareness expressed in the cry 'A different world is possible!'

This counterbalance of a global public opinion corresponds to the new age of our planetary world which has to take account of the interdependence of states, another conception of their sovereignty, the right to interfere, the International Court of Human Rights, and the urgent need for a world government.

In the reflections which follow I want to emphasize the contribution of Christianity to the emergence of a different possible world. I shall begin by meditating on the profound ambiguity of a history marked by globalization. Then I want to recall God's dream of history. Here we note that the human countenance is inseparable from the divine countenance witnessed to by Jesus in the gospel. Then we shall consider in what direction the Christian churches can work to transform the 'possibilities of history' into realities. What I call a possibility stands at the point of contact between a historical destiny and human freedom when confronted with a creative initiative. But nothing unprecedented can emerge on the horizon of history without a magnetic attraction. So what initiatives can Christians take under the magnetic force of the gospel?

I. A profoundly ambiguous history

More than ever, history is marked by ambiguity. The future course of the third millennium which is now beginning cannot be foreseen. We have become sceptical about all optimistic philosophies and even theologies of history. The process of desacralization and secularization which coincided with the advent of modernity understood as a victory of critical reason engendered a tremendous hope in the unlimited possibilities of scientific and technological progress to triumph over the disasters of history and to improve the human condition. But above all in view of the cruel twentieth century just past, faith in rational projects has been seriously shaken. Modernity has not kept its promises; instead, the famous disenchantment with the world has led to disenchantment even with the myth of progress.

The secular religion of a classless society experienced a resounding setback with the collapse of Soviet Marxism. The pagan religion of race led to the worst failure of reason and Western civilization with the catastrophe of Auschwitz. Furthermore, despite prodigious conquests, the men and women of the third millennium are having more and more difficulties in coping with the perverse effects of technology and science. We know the alarming conclusions of experts on the environment, genetic manipulation and ecological devastation. In particular we can no longer control global warming. For the first time in the long history of humankind, human scientific mastery and technology is such that the very future of the human species and the planetary village, our earth, is in our hands. Either we shall have the wisdom to modify ongoing processes or we shall all perish. That is why our historical responsibility relates not only to the conditions of a harmonious life in tomorrow's societies, but to the ongoing existence of an authentically human life on earth.

So more than ever, history is marked by ambiguity. But those who talk of ambiguity say that we must leave the future open and not give way to an apocalyptic view of history. As the French thinker Edgar Morin is fond of saying, 'the improbable is possible'. Happily the darkest forecasts of the experts are proved wrong. This can be seen, for example, in connection with the supposed impossibility of controlling the galloping growth of the world's population. We must not despair of the promise of human genius to remedy the perverse effects of progress in the sphere of pollution, the struggle against hunger, and bring victory in pandemics like AIDS. We do not know the infinite resources of human liberty when it is mobilized to reverse the fatal course of human history.

This is all the more true when we remember that humanity has entered a planetary age which is also that of globalization. The very ambiguity of history on the threshold of the third millennium is that of the phenomenon of globalization. It depends on the good will of men and women whether they bring about the worst or favour the best. It has to be noted that, as the global system is functioning at present along the lines of the free market, it is generating misery for three-quarters of humankind. Who can accept with resignation that 20 per cent of the global population owns 83 per cent of the disposable riches of the world, while the 20 per cent who are the poorest have to survive on 1.4 per cent of natural resources? How can we bear to think that at the beginning of the twenty-first century 14 million children are dying each year before the age of five? And over and above this blatant injustice, through an ever-expanding global network the dehumanizing consequences of a certain uniform model of culture (call it cultural Macdonaldism) are spreading to the whole of the planet and eroding away the original local cultures.

However, this deadly consequence of globalization is not a disaster. Those who dream of a different world can see how it should be possible to exploit the real possibilities of the phenomenon of globalization within the planetary village. In fact the human family has become aware of its unity in a new way. It is showing solidarity in the face of its destiny, and the necessary inter-dependence of states and the speed of exchanging information are encouraging the emergence of a universal awareness of the need to defend human rights and the rights of the earth. In the face of the structural disorder of the global market, ecological catastrophes, the systematic violence of the rights of persons and the jealous sovereignty of states will have to give way to the supra-national sovereignty of the global community. Not only has our view of history gone beyond a post-colonial Western ethnocentricity, but we can no longer consider history as a history of freedoms apart from the history of planet earth and indeed of the whole cosmos.

II. God's dream of history

Faced with the fundamental ambiguity of history, as Christians we have no secret information about the outcome of the human adventure or the destiny of planet earth, lost in the vastness of the cosmos. But in faith we know at least God's dream when he took the risk of making created freedoms arise out of the void. Human existence is simply a function of this absolute future which is life in and with God. It is precisely this hope which gives human history its value and its importance. Despite its inscrutable character, history is tending towards its fulfilment when the kingdom of God will be 'all in all'. Something beyond history relativizes every concrete realization in this world.

But history is other than the outward framework of our spiritual adventure in the order of love. It is a history of salvation in the strong sense, not only as a vital exchange with God, but as a healing of the whole human being and creation itself as a habitable earth. Here God is making himself an accomplice of time to realize his creative plan for human beings to the point of assuming the human condition in Jesus Christ in order to triumph over death and every form of death. The remembrance of Christ died and risen is the radical foundation of the Christian hope in the face of the unknowns of history.

All the religions are in their own way religions of salvation, at least in the sense that they seek to cure human beings of their finitude and promise them an immortality beyond death. It is this that makes Christianity unique among the religions of the world and it is this that is the basis of our confidence in the future of Christianity, despite some quantitative and qualitative decline of the institutional churches, above all in the West. There is a deep bond between Christianity as a religion and authentic humanity. At the heart of Christianity lies the paradox of the incarnation, the future of God in human beings. From now on the countenance of God and the human countenance are inseparable. Over the centuries and more precisely since the 1215 Lateran Council, our theological thought was above all concerned to assert 'the greatest possible dissimilarity between God and man'. Today, as a result of the threats which lie over the future of humankind, we must meditate seriously on the ever greater humanity of God and God's way of dealing with our inhumanity.

In his reinterpretation of the religion of Israel, Jesus put an end to the violence of the sacred, not only the sacred of human rituals but also the sacred of a God who is still violent, a wholly other God who defines himself above all in terms of omnipotence, perfection and eternity. If Christianity is faithful to its own genius and to the religion of Jesus, then it can be a religion with a boundless future which links up with the hope of freedom from the violence of the sacred in every human being through which it is also possible to mitigate the violence of history.

For too long Christian thought, at the very moment when it has emphasized the purely temporal character of the messianism of Israel, has excessively spiritualized the messianism of Jesus, as if it had no real bearing on the course of history. In the face of the blatant injustices and indeed the crimes in recent history, it is the merit of the practice and thought of the church and of the second half of the twentieth century to have rediscovered the messianic dimension of Christianity, i.e. the power to transform history which implies the announcement of the kingdom of God in word and deed. Exegetes and theologians have shown in particular how the eschatology of the New Testament transforms the promises of the First Testament, which announces the future of a kingdom of justice and peace on earth without abolishing them. The kingdom proclaimed by Jesus is not of this world, but it can already have its anticipation in the course of history.

Certainly the messianism of Jesus is paradoxical because it ends in the failure of the cross. Jesus does not repel the violence of history, but is its victim. But precisely in his death he shows up in a prophetic way that only non-violence can put an end to the ever-recurring cycle of violence. Does that mean that the church is condemned to impotence in the face of human justice, while waiting for God's judgment? No, because the memory of Christ is a dangerous memory for all those who make themselves accomplices of the powers of evil.

The preferential option for the poor proclaimed by the church of Latin America is tending to become the option of all the churches, above all in Africa and Asia. And it is a good indication that the Christian hope for something beyond history is no stranger to the concrete hopes of all the oppressed. As I have already said, human liberation is an integral part of salvation. It is the historical responsibility of all the disciples of Jesus (Christians, but also all men and women who live out the spirit of Jesus without knowing it) to give history a human face. But in imitating Jesus, they know that they cannot make justice and peace triumph by using the weapons of power and violence.

III. Writing a history with a human face: the possibilities of history

The global meaning of history escapes us, but we already give a meaning to every fragment of history whenever we struggle alongside all men and women of good will against injustice and absurdity. The church does not have a magical recipe for building a different, fairer, world which is more pleasant to live in. But the future remains open, and the foundation of Christian hope is the certainty that the Spirit of God is still at work to renew the face of the earth. Every time we put the practices of Jesus to work as practices of liberation and humanization, we give a human face to history and we anticipate the kingdom of God among human beings.

I began by referring to the 'possibilities of history', that is to say promises which can become realities if Christians are capable of creative initiatives in faithfulness to the gospel. I would like to suggest four directions which could help towards the emergence of a different possible world.

1. A purification of the memory

A retrospect on twenty centuries of Christianity shows us – alongside admirable actions – how ineffective in practice the ideal of the gospel has been; it has not made enough of a mark on the course of history. There are not only the lost opportunities, the schisms in Christianity, the Crusades, the exclusion of the Jews, the wars of religion, the treatment of blacks, but also the perversion of the gospel in the name of the defence of the truth and of missionary conquest. It is the merit of the church of John Paul II that it has invited Christians to the work of purifying the memory and that it has begun to take a way of repentance and conversion. But this approach has a future only if it is accompanied by historical discernment of the causes which have encouraged these deviations from the Christian ideal.

In particular we must ask about the false legitimation of proselytism in the name of the absolute rights of revealed truth that scorns the rights of the conscience. We have not yet finished meditating on the scope of the Vatican II Declaration on Religious Freedom, which proclaims that 'the truth can be imposed only by the force of the truth'. It is in this context that we must welcome as a sign of the times the new dialogue between the religions. Over and above their ancestral quarrels, the religions are understanding better that they are not there to be at their own service but must serve the great causes which prod the universal human conscience. Above all in the face of the current challenges of globalization, inter-religious dialogue has the opportunity to encourage a reciprocal emulation of religions to serve peace and the slow emergence of a global community which is more worth living in.

2. Respect for true humanity

In the face of the dangers of dehumanization during the current process of globalization, the witnesses to the gospel have a vocation to create a counter-culture, and must work with others to seek and promote authentic humanity. We still do not have a very good knowledge of what this true humanity is, what the Vatican II constitution *Gaudium et spes* called the *vere humanum*.

But we know increasingly well the abysses of which human beings are capable. In modern and pluralist societies the church can no longer claim to impose its ethical programme in an authoritarian way, but must continue to bear witness forcefully to its vision of humanity, in discussion with other moral and political authorities.

In the face of the formidable questions which are arising and the global economic disorder which is being produced by new technologies in the order of the reproduction of human life, we urgently feel the need for a global ethic on a planetary scale. The dialogue of the great religions is already a positive element for the future of the global community. But the tentative quest for an alternative world is also bound up with the need to address the question of the relationship between morals with a religious foundation and secular ethics. All the religions, beginning with Christianity, must listen to the calls of the universal human conscience and the legitimate aspirations of men and women of the third millennium in terms of freedom and happiness. I would even dare to say that all the religions which are in fact inhuman in their doctrines or their practices must serious reinterpret their basic texts and their traditions. Conversely, purely secular ethical authorities must take into account the wisdom of the religious traditions in their view of humanity. It is by no means certain that the purely hedonistic ethic focussed on consumption conveyed by the media is a help towards the arrival of a globalization with a human face. It is the responsibility of the believers of the three great monotheistic religions in particular to show that there is no fatal contradiction between the quest for a personal God and respect for true humanity.

3. The law of superabundance

Many Christians ask themselves how original their witness and their action is, in that they have no monopoly of initiatives towards justice and solidarity. They have to rejoice in particular at the success of humanitarian action above all among the young. And it is true that in our secularized society there are still many good people who are ready at least to respect the Golden Rule: 'Do not do to others that you would not want them to do to you.' It is almost as if the quasi-religion of human rights had taken over from the ancient historical religions.

Now the crimes against humanity committed in our current history should be enough to convince us of the fragility of the human conscience left to its inner demons. It is becoming increasingly evident that even in the so-called constitutional states a society which is ruled only by the strictest rules of justice is rapidly becoming oppressive. It needs to be replaced by a culture of love and peace. In a word, there is a need to go back beyond the rules of justice, which are the rules of equivalence, to another logic, that of the law of superabundance which takes us back to the paradox of the gospel. A different world is possible if we take account of this logic of gratuitous love, of forgiveness, of compassion, which ensures that over and beyond the strict equity of justice the scales tip in favour of the disadvantaged. In any case it is the surest way of writing a history with a human face that works secretly towards the kingdom of God.

4. An ecological justice

For the first time, we are discovering that it is not enough to defend human rights unless at the same time we respect the rights of the earth. Some people are already talking of the possibility of ecological justice and even of an ecological globalization. The powers of science and technology are in fact such that we can commit crimes against the identity of the human genome and against the balances which safeguard a sustainable human life on earth. The emission of greenhouse gases is not ceasing to grow, while the United States is still refusing to ratify the Kyoto agreement. The key question for tomorrow's world is the self-limitation of human power. How can we ward off the perverse effects of what today we are experiencing as progress? How can we ensure that the earth is still habitable for generations to come? One is tempted to recall the new moral imperative put forward by Hans Jonas in his book on the principle of responsibility: 'Act in such a way that the effects of your action are compatible with the permanence of an authentically human life on earth.'

In the face of the possibility of an ecological catastrophe on a planetary scale, our spontaneous confidence in the future, in life, in being, must be relaunched by our confidence in the God of the biblical tradition. It is the human vocation to be co-creators with God and to make the world habitable. But the transformation and exploitation of the resources of the earth must not give way to the vertigo of a Promethean excess. Just as God rested on the seventh day, so men and women of the third millennium must learn a sabbatical wisdom, that of gratuitousness, restraint, silence, praise and marvel at creation. This is not a luxury reserved for just some. It is a matter of survival when confronted with the blank page of history.

Translated by John Bowden

God on the Side of Justice and the Poor?

ÉLOI MESSI METOGO

The word 'God' in the title does not have a specific religious meaning. It denotes the supreme reality on which religions focus through myths and beliefs, rites and norms of behaviour. This reality is called God, Allah, the Absolute, Nirvana, Shunyata, Dao, Amma, Nzaambi Puungu Magani, Ngül Mpwo, etc., depending on the tradition. As Hans Küng puts it, this transcendence is situated 'above or within, in space and/or time, as redemption, illumination or liberation'. It is worth noting that in black Africa, which determines my perspective, what counts generally in religious traditions is not the being of the supreme reality, but – for want of a less ambiguous term – 'salvation'. The important thing is to be delivered from the forces of evil, to restore the bonds which unite the members of the community, to rediscover communion with one's ancestors. Salvation consists in enjoying good health, substantial material goods and a large family, and in succeeding in what one undertakes. According to Henri Maurier, 'the idea of God and of immortality remain fluid . . . the only realistic aim is life in this world in a family which is made up of a series of generations. The ancestors, signs of continued success in the past, become the vehicles of demands for the future.'[1]

In general, this conception of salvation determines how religions from elsewhere are received, the most important of these being Islam and Christianity (the latter essentially in its Protestant and Catholic versions). The Far Eastern religions are also present, and the doctrine of reincarnation attracts Christians who think that their church has hidden this 'truth' from them. Mention needs also to be made of Gnostic currents which fascinate many people in a particularly difficult social and economic context. The chief of these are the Rosicrucians and New Age, which inspire small groups like the Grail and the Way, and syncretistic movements like Baha'i. However, these movements commandeer the person of Jesus and the fundamental dogmas of Christianity to reinterpret them in systems in which human beings are thought to arrive at knowledge of the deity through their own efforts and not by a revelation, or in the quest for a synthesis of all religions. One reason why secret societies are attractive is because people want to be introduced into an influential network in order to get a job or be promoted in their profession.

More than twenty years ago, in his famous book *Le Cri de l'homme africain*,[2] Jean-Marc Ela wrote that religion cannot be considered purely and simply as the opium of the African peoples. It is impossible to deny that religious resources were mobilized in the fight of, say, Chaka or Samory against the Western colonial invasion. From the first phase of the evangelization of sub-Saharan Africa in the fifteenth and sixteenth centuries and down to the middle of the twentieth century, we can see the appearance of separatist movements with a political and religious character. In South Africa, where apartheid held sway, 'prophets' protested against the exploitation of the blacks, where politics or racial segregation even extended to worship. They challenged the confiscation of Jesus and his message by the ideologists of racial superiority and white civilization. Such a Christ needed to be replaced by a 'black Christ', close to Africans, capable of sharing their pains and sufferings and helping them to liberate themselves. In the Belgian Congo, for example, Simon Kimbangu, who received a vision and was influenced by black Americans opposed to racial segregation, based himself on the Bible to claim the dignity and freedom of his people. He died in prison in 1951.

The majority of the prophetic movements became independent churches after the deaths of their founders and were suppressed by the colonialists to the point that they could express themselves only in the religious sphere; in this way they lost their revolutionary character in the political regimes after independence. Éric de Rosny suggests that they should be located in the Pentecostalism which has spread widely in black Africa. At least three features shared by the Afro-Christian churches and the Pentecostal movements have been noted: visions at the calling of most of the preachers (among the Pentecostals the fruits of the presence of the Spirit can also be seen in those who hear the good news); healings in which victory over the disease and the demon responsible for it is manifested; the interpretation of the Bible solely under the inspiration of the Holy Spirit. At all events, emphasis is put on exorcism and prayers for healing. The liberal Catholic Church and the Gallican church also devote themselves to a ministry of healing; Jehovah's Witnesses spread stories of visions and healings to attract members; and the Christian Scientists, more Gnostic in their theology, offer prayers of healing rather than medicine from hospitals, which they say is useless.

Many Africans, whether adherents of the traditional religions, Christians (of all denominations) or Muslims, regard religion as a bulwark against poverty and sickness. In a Christian context they do not welcome priests and pastors who will not practise exorcism or lay their hands on the sick. We can ask with Éric de Rosny whether we must not wait 'until the theologies of healing take over from liberation theologies', if the religions which take the desire for healing most into account are not to experience the greatest growth.

Apart from the powers of divination and healing attributed to the marabouts, we should note that Islam is opposed to the colonial powers, and that today it is shaping civil society in its resistance to state domination.[3] Through aid associations and legal alms (*zakat*), it is organizing a 'counter-society or a parallel society which obstinately evades the state'.[4] The Muslim leader defends the peasants against the authorities, and the Muslim tradition of solidarity, concern for the poor and justice encourages the struggle of industrial workers through trade unions or the revolt of marginalized youth.

We can see how religion has constituted and still constitutes a bulwark for the poor and weak in Africa, and we can also note this in other parts of the world. But the poor and the weak are not the only ones to resort to 'God', and the way in which they do so often raises questions about the 'salvation' that they expect.

Politicians often resort to the traditional religions (or what remains of them in terms of institutions) to consolidate their power. Thus a head of state will 'invest in' or 'get support from' an ethnic religious organization. There is above all an insidious way of perpetuating and exploiting the cult of ancestors, though this is harmed by urbanization, school and the media, which favour the autonomy of the individual, criticism of tradition, and what Alain Marie calls the 'communitarian despotism'[5] of traditional hierarchical societies. The state, first the colonial state and then the post-colonial state, is built up on the model of communitarian despotism. Political and economic power belong to the elders. The head of state is called 'father of the nation' and preaches dialogue and peace, which are the 'modern translations of the communitarian consensus'.[6] In principle, the elders in power should redistribute the wealth and resources they accumulate to the younger generation, and this in return owes them respect and obedience. It is unthinkable that the young should show opposition: that would make them ungrateful 'children', victims of 'their bad "individualist" drives'". In reality, when redistributions do take place, they are selective and cannot therefore cover the needs of all. Basically the majority of African rulers commandeer the instruments of modernity (bureaucratic state, science, technology, market economy, media) for their sole benefit, while imposing on a destitute people talk of returning to the sources and to authenticity. In the 1950s one saw political parties formed on the basis of traditional secret societies like the Poro in West Africa. These traditional references are now backed up by membership of the Rosicrucians or Freemasonry, which binds together the majority of current state powers.

The bishops write fierce pastoral letters against corruption, the misappropriation of public funds, the absence of democracy and the violation of human rights. Unfortunately these texts are almost unknown to the wider public and are not the object of any debate. Moreover the signatories do not renounce their ambiguous relations with the circles in power and this can only blunt the possible impact of the documents at episcopal conferences. Here we can speak of the compromise of religion with political power. But this language falls short of the problem raised by Islam in general as a religion which reinforces state projects. The rise of Islam in Nigeria, Niger and Chad is disturbing in what it means for human rights, both for Muslims themselves and for non-Muslims. This leads me to mention briefly Jewish, Christian and Muslim integralism and fundamentalism. Without doing away with the notable differences between the elements of each of the two groups, Jean Louis Schlegel distinguishes between Catholic and Jewish integralists and Protestant and Muslim fundamentalists.[7] What all have in common, among other things, is 'a political vision which they want to impose on everyone'; however, integralists and fundamentalists 'are distinguished by their point of reference: for the former it is the tradition, or rather a moment given by tradition (the nineteenth century for Catholics, the ghetto period for the ultra-Orthodox Jews); for the latter it is the scriptures, the origin read literally as if there was an initial moment preserved from any interpertation'.[8] Despite the political support that the ultra-Orthodox Jews have brought either to Likud or to Labour over the decades, the integralists are not really a danger on a social and religious level. They are dissident sectarian groups which do not threaten the cohesion of the larger religious group. By contrast, 'the fundamentalists represent an offshoot, a tendency within the major religious group itself; they are co-extensive with this group to the point that no one could say clearly today where Protestant and Muslim fundamentalists begin and where they end. Moreover, the spectrum of fundamentalism ranges from very moderate people who are ignored as such, to radical activists and indeed a very small minority which is ready to resort to violence. It is precisely this characteristic – of being a tendency with a following wind and coextensive with the whole of their a group – which makes up the particular danger posed by fundamentalists today.'⁹

While Protestant fundamentalists stand in the democratic tradition as far as politics is concerned, integralists and fundamentalists largely reject the essential achievements of modernity: the separation of religion from politics, the autonomy of reason, democracy, limitless criticism and in particular criticism of religion. They think the notion of 'human rights' wicked and thus unacceptable. Human beings do not have rights but only responsibilities towards God, as laid down in scripture or tradition. One finds happiness by fulfilling these scrupulously. According to a direct reading of the scriptures (Bible or Qur'an), power comes directly from God and does not allow either discussion or debate. As Schlegel observes, the expression 'Islamic republic' is a contradiction in terms, since 'public affairs' have been taken over by Islam. No constitutional or legal ruling allows the control of the exercise of power or an assignation of limits to it.

We can say that today the great religions of the world (I am thinking in particular of the monotheistic Abraham religions of Judaism, Christianity and Islam) are assets for development, justice and peace. I would add that the so-called tribal religions, which are often treated with scorn, also have resources of this kind, if only because they ignore proselytism and the struggle for influence. As well as ecumenical meetings like that in Assisi in 1986 and theological debates among experts, there are specific individual and collective engagements. However, it would be good to see responsible religious Jews distancing themselves from the politics of Ariel Sharon and Protestants doing the same from their extremist fellow-religionists in Ulster. On the Catholic side, it is to be feared that an alliance with Muslims against contraceptives and the pill only gives the impression that eyes are being closed to the absence of democracy and the violation of human rights in Muslim countries. Moreover, and this affects Christian churches in the Third World, social and charitable work of undisputed value should not relegate to a second level or totally eclipse a critique of unjust political and economic systems. There is also a need to see that charitable activities do not benefit only the well-to-do, above all in the case of hospitals, schools and institutions of higher education.

It is disturbing that there is often a considerable gap between the openness of religious heads, theologians and intellectuals towards religious tolerance, ecumenical dialogue and the quest for peace, and the self-centredness, sectarianism and conservativism of the communities or a large number of their members. While in Africa a kind of lived-out ecumenism is bringing together adherents of different religions in a large number of families, this coexistence is threatened by the rise of Islam and the multiplication of often intolerant new churches.

Integralism and fundamentalism are undoubtedly the expression of the perplexity of many of our contemporaries when faced with the rational criticism of religion, the economic crisis and the enigmas and uncertainties of life. The question remains what the proposed responses are worth. The political instrumentalization of God leads to violence and injustice, while the immediate recourse to supernatural powers to find a job and regain health does not change the condition of the poor in any way, because there is no analysis of the mechanisms which bring poverty and domination with a view to effective political actions. Those who fish in troubled waters – and these are usually those among the poor who are more cunning than others – exploit popular credulity by covering themselves with the mantle of religion. There are now countless false priests and healers.

Where is God? Whose side is he on? According the Cameroon philosopher and theologian Fabien Eboussi Boulaga, in the strategy of life '"God" can be used as an offensive force to attack, surprise, dissimulate, deceive, compel and wear down. "God" can also be used as a defensive force to ward off, repel, evade, protect, break, disengage and threaten.'[10] In the struggle against death, all resort to God – rich and poor, just and unjust alike. One of the important questions about religion today is beyond question whether and how one can resort to God without eliminating others and losing oneself.

Translated by John Bowden

Notes

1. H. Maurier, *La Religion spontanée, Philosophie des religions d'Afrique noire*, Paris 1997, pp. 75–6.
2. Paris 1980.
3. See Christian Coulon, *Les Musulmans et le pouvoir en Afrique noire*, Paris 1988.
4. Ibid., p.76.
5. Alain Marie (ed.), *L'Afrique des individus*, Paris 1997, p. 67.
6. Ibid., p.91.
7. 'Les religions, obstacles ou atouts pour le développement?', *Foi et Développement* 324, Paris, May 2004, on which I draw for what follows.
8. Ibid., p.7.
9. Ibid.
10. *À contretemps, L'enjeu de Dieu en Afrique*, Paris 1991, p. 214.

III. How can a Different World Be Sustained?

Searching for David's Sling:
Tapping the Local Resources of Hope

The empire, globalization, hierarchy and hegemonic universalism – these are some of the major challenges today for subordinated peoples all over the world. We do not have commensurate instruments and mechanism at the global level to come to terms with these dreadful realities. But there is always a David in human history. The future of the victims and their hope for a different world lies in the search for the sling in their resources and in their resilience in the midst of what appears at this moment as a hopeless situation for themselves and for all humanity.

I. The mood of disenchantment

In a contribution to a conference recently held in the University of Seville, Fred Dallmayr invokes the reaction of an international judicial luminary to the way Saddam Hussein was displayed before the world press and TV screens 'shackled and dishevelled'.[1] This is 'pretty much what the Roman Emperors used to do to defeated barbarian kings'. In a melancholy tone he adds that things have remained much the same since the time of Caesar in spite of 'Christian civilization'.

I think it would be more accurate to say that humanity did make efforts to rise up and move forward in civility, but that events like the wars on Afghanistan and Iraq have thrown us back to the abyss, raising basic questions about humanity, its survival and its future, especially for its weaker ones. The reason is not far to seek: we live in a period in which empire and globalization, hierarchy and justificatory universalism rule the day. The net result is the creation of a world gripped in insecurity and devoid of hope. This is true as much of the developed world as the developing ones, though it originates from different sources.

It is interesting to note that the insecurity caused by the plague in medieval Europe led people, as Norman Cantor notes, to the search for pleasures precisely because all that they had was the present, and no one knew what could happen the next moment.[2] Today's culture of consumerism and pursuit of pleasure are symptoms of deep insecurity, and not of contentment and hope.[3] For instance, the frustration deriving from the sheer lack of a job among the unemployed, and the fear among the employed of being thrown out at any moment with no future prospects, are deeply worrying. In developing countries, the volatile and unjust political situation and the negation of the bare necessities of life drive people to have recourse to terrorist suicides or starvation suicides – in both cases, the root cause is simply desperation.

Could the utopias of the past come to our aid? Unfortunately the answer has to be in the negative. The disenchantment with many past utopias is due to the fact that, while they mystify human consciousness, they were unable to move the victims towards a realistic goal, and in terms of strategy they were steered by elites who claimed to represent the people – while in fact, most often they did not – and even exploited them for their power and vested interests, as the dynamics of many revolutions have borne witness.

II. The onslaught of a conservative 'revolution'

It appears to me that globalization today is playing the same kind of mythical role that revolution did in the past, and could be considered as its functional equivalent. Writing the history of the Russian Revolution, Leon Trotsky observed that 'the most indubitable feature of a revolution is the direct interference of the masses in historic events . . . The history of a revolution is for us first of all a history of the forcible entrance of the masses into the realm of rulership over their destiny.'[4] Despite the cosmetic use of modern terminologies, globalization as a project is a conservative revolution taking the world to the restoration of capitalism without restraint.[5] It is not a revolution of the people, but is manufactured for the people by others who reap the benefit, as the tyranny and terror that followed many a revolution in the past amply demonstrate.

Globalization is a mystification which is naked violence dressed up in respectable apparel for public appeal. It could hardly be as much a matter of hope as the past revolutions were for the ordinary people. I think that in these circumstances, to advocate globalization as the new-found hope for the developing countries would be tantamount to Spain advising Switzerland to invest its entire wherewithal to build up a strong navy to defend itself!

III. The loss of legacies and the poor as defenders of reason and humaneness

A pall of gloom envelops humanity as some of the important achievements of its centuries-long struggle are thrown to the winds overnight. The Universal Declaration of Human Rights (1948) which the United Nations saw as the 'common standard of achievement for all peoples and all nations' is at serious risk today. International law and conventions on the treatment of prisoners and under-trials have been eroded by the claim of exceptionalism by the empire. In the realm of labour, the struggles waged by the working class for their legitimate rights and security of employment for the past 150 years are being nullified by the casualization of labour, which is a pliable form of domination.[6] Social entitlements no longer have a place. All are to be surrendered on the altar of the empire and the market, or so it would seem.

These legacies are being replaced with strange logic and opportune ideologies. As in the past, the present empire too is based on ideological justification for its domination. We are all witnesses to the unabashed and routine explanation of 'collateral damage' after the murder of innocents, and the dogma of the 'pre-emptive strike' as *causa belli*. Such ideological shibboleths of the empire have lost credibility. The victims have begun to realize through their native wisdom that the concern of the empire and liberal capitalism for the poor is as real as the tears of the wolf seeing the lamb getting wet in the rain.

In the face of such developments, when even international institutions are unable to restrain the course of events, much less challenge them, for the victims there remains no other means than to turn to their rich local resources to keep burning the flame of hope and dream for a different world. In a world in which the empire, globalization, hierarchy and hegemonic universalism are at work, ironically, the poor through their resistance have become the defenders of reason by unmasking the abuse of power and its arbitrariness by the empire as it desperately tries to cover its moral nakedness with a semblance of reason. In their own way, and with local intellectual and cultural resources, the victims question what is taken to be self-evident, namely, that there is no alternative to the present model of economy, and that maximization of profit is the ultimate human happiness. They also challenge the divorce between the economic and social which serves to bury the ideal of the welfare state.

Felix Wilfred

IV. The well-springs of humanity

By turning to their own local resources, people respond to the crisis that envelops their daily lives, and the destiny of humanity at large. I do not think that events like the World Social Forum or the dramatic protest at Seattle against WTO have the capacity either to pull down the empire or to arrest globalization. However, they have high symbolic value, and new symbols are the need of the hour. These events represent the confluence of many streams of dissent, protest springing from local sources to form a mighty river.

The local resources invite us to direct our attention to the deep humanity inherent in human beings which goes beyond considerations of one's advantages and profits, and beyond the ideology of competence. I am reminded of a parable of Mencius, the disciple of Confucius. If a child were on the brink of falling into a well, we would spontaneously reach out to save it. And we would do so not to win public acclaim or to merit the gratitude of the parents of the child.[7] It would be simply something which the humanity deep down within us impelled us to do. The local resources of ordinary people is replete with deep humanity, and they have found expression in their practices of daily life, their stories, songs, proverbs and so on.

Affluence creates a weak person and a fragile culture. On the other hand, the confrontation with human suffering and response in terms of compassion has developed in the victims some of the values we require to sustain a different world – solidarity, humaneness, the spirit of sharing, the technique of survival, readiness to take risks, endurance and steely determination in the midst of adversities. In the world of the victims, unlike in the world of the empire and globalisation, the good does not get identified with the 'successful'. The good and the just are ideals the world needs relentlessly to strive after. Some of these values and perceptions have become crystallized in their culture of everyday life. Their cultural resources reflecting the values and ideals of a future world help them to face their lives with courage at individual and collective levels.

V. Generating hope – the dynamics of resistance

The hope for tomorrow lies in the resistance of today. But resistance against the empire and globalization often assume an ambivalent character. On the one hand there is the practical necessity to comply with the existing order of things; on the other, there is the refusal to surrender and acquiesce to the inevitable. What appears as compliance out of the need to survive co-exists with the practice of resistance. At an individual level, Galileo exemplifies this situation, and he is a metaphor for the plight of the subordinated peoples. While he had to assent outwardly to the view that the earth does not move, something which the infamous Roman Inquisition demanded of him, his spirit triumphed when at the conclusion of the trial he whispered sotto voce *'e pur si muove'* (. . . and yet it moves). In most local traditions, we have the example of an interplay of acquiescence and resistance.

The resistance may not be always open, but it is there, and it manifests itself in innumerable ways and forms in daily life. This is true of the way the *dalits* (the untouchables) in South Asia respond to caste-hierarchy and its oppression,[8] and the peasants in Malaysia resist the exacting landlords. After extensive field study on the modes of resistance by Malay peasants, James Scott observes:

> They [Malay peasants] require little or no coordination or planning; they make use of implicit understandings and informal networks; they often represent a form of individual self-help; they typically avoid any direct, symbolic confrontation with authority . . . It is my guess that just such kind of resistance are often the most significant and the most effective over the long run . . . Everyday forms of resistance make no headlines. But just as millions of anthozoan polyps create, willy-nilly, a coral reef, so do the multiple acts of peasant insubordination and evasion create political and economic barrier reefs of their own.[9]

This dynamic of resistance that has been present for millennia at the local level in the various civilizations is now being enacted on the larger global stage. The fact that people accommodate to globalization does not mean that we could project it as the future of the world. For deep down there is another dynamic at work, namely that of resistance. The resistance derives from the experience of the woeful effects of globalization and empire on their daily lives; it also stems from the realization of the absence of humane ideals and noble values in the present oppressive order. The forms which it takes at the macro-level reflect local resources and experiences, as could be witnessed in the protest against WTO or in the events of World Social Forum to which I referred earlier.

Arundhati Roy, who has been a fearless voice today against the power of the empire and its warmongering, shows how the small people with their resources can resist the empire and thus move into the realm of hope. In her address at the closing rally of the World Social Forum at Porto Alegre, she said that what we need to do is 'to lay siege to it [empire], to shame it, to mock it: with our art, our music, our literature, our stubbornness, our joy, our brilliance, our sheer relentlessness – and our ability to tell our own stories'.[10] These 'weapons of the weak' obviously will not either bring the empire tumbling down or arrest the march of globalization. But they have a power which comes from human ingenuity and resourcefulness that neither armaments nor economic power can withstand for long.

In March this year, while visiting South Africa, where Gandhi woke up to the harsh reality of racial oppression, I read the voluminous autobiography of Nelson Mandela, *Long Walk to Freedom*.[11] The book fascinated me immensely and made me realize what tapping of local resources means, and how local leaders with utopian dreams are formed and shaped. Apartheid was something unique, and Mandela, this colossus of a statesman from rural Africa, could mobilize the resources, symbols and strategies from the land to fight an oppressive regime. The way in which this iron-fisted system was loosened and finally dismantled shows us the importance of sustained dissent and protest in confronting systems of power and the efficacy of local resources.

VI. Cleopatra's nose and the course of history

It is an irony that some of the ideas and justificatory frames of thought discarded long ago reappear in new avatars. One such is historical determinism as it appears in the work of Francis Fukuyama. What he has done is to carry to an extreme formulation the underlying sentiments of the votaries of neoliberalism. In effect, the claim that the final phase of human history has arrived with the triumph of capitalism is a form of determinism bordering on fatalism, and is not very different from the one which invoked the will of God for the justification of unjustifiable injustices, and for the legitimacy of oppressive institutional orders. Such claims do not allow any room for the agency of the subordinated peoples and the capacity of the victims of our history to imagine alternatives and a different order of things. The victims are confronted once again with what seems to be the recurrent myopia of all empires and systems, namely to believe that with them the human history has reached its apogee.

The grand deterministic scheme of universal history projected by Hegel is the last thing the marginalized people are prepared to believe in (no wonder that Isaiah Berlin has placed Hegel among the six enemies of freedom!).[12] For him, history is the history of winners and those who are successful; the losers and victims have no place. Francis Fukuyama seems to suffer under the weight of this tradition. The new historical credo is nothing but market and liberalism, and all that the 'wretched of the earth' have to say is 'Amen'. But this is not what the victims of history are going to do, if we go by the ground swell of resistance and protests from every corner of the world to the prevailing order of things.

The hope of the marginal peoples rests on a different conception of history and its future. Local experiences and wisdom tell that history is incalculable and full of imponderables. In their scheme of things, history is not a concatenation of predictable events following the scheme of cause and effect. Science, on the basis of available data, makes projections for a future which is different from hope that of another order. Subordinated peoples rely on hope which is tied up with moral reason and emancipation. Hope breaks the cycle of reasoning in terms of cause and effect, and creates room for surprises and the unknown. For the subordinated peoples and victims hope is kindled by the experience of indignity, suffering, deprivation and injustice. No one believes any more in the unpredictable character of history as the marginalized of our world. This belief leads them to refuse to equate the inevitable with the just.

How ordinary people keep alive the hope in spite of all projections to the contrary is illustrated by an Indian proverb that says 'There are a thousand suns beyond the clouds'. It inspired the title for a captivating book on hope by the well-known French journalist Dominique Lapierre.[13] The insights of ancient historians like Thucydides and modern thinkers like Pascal converge in the same direction. If only Cleopatra's nose had been a little shorter, world history would have taken a different course, and if only Cromwell had not had that little piece of sand-grain in his bladder, the face of Europe would have been completely different.[14] The poor of the earth can live much more comfortably with insecurities, trusting in a different course of history from that of the elites who would like the history to be nothing but the replication of the present, for fear of the unknown.

VII. Countering the hegemonic universal

Like history, the marginal peoples have another conception of the universal. In fact, the future of our world and its hope lie in the resistance of the subordinated peoples to the prevailing conception of the universals. The empire, globalization and hierarchy seem to share the same kind of under-standing of the universal: it is an expansionist and assimilationist view that denies the subjecthood of peoples and ignores difference and pluralism. Universality, obviously, is not to be confounded with ubiquity. Organized greed and selfishness could be present everywhere in the world, as is happening with the expansion of capitalism and market, but it does not mean that they could qualify to be universal, which is basically a spiritual quality of transcendence.

True universality is possible only where there is sacrifice and renunciation. The ability to accept the other, moving out of one's cultural, ideological, national or ethnic cocoon, will mark the quality of universality. Therefore the universal could be present very much at the local level in the experience of subordinated peoples, the illiterate villagers and powerless identities; it could be glaringly absent among the well-to-do living in metropolises bent on themselves with little regard for the other. The poor are attuned to the spirit of genuine universality promising hope for our world, while the worldwide expansion of selfish pursuit is not. The latter is the enemy of universality.

VIII. The art of negotiating the borders

From a historical point of view, we know that no civilization or culture developed in isolation, but always in a movement of give and take.[15] We see this best exemplified at the grassroots in the lives of the poor. Theirs is basically a world-view in which the borders are porous and always negotiable, and could be reconstituted ever anew, as so many micro-studies indicate. They have also developed cultural resources for communication and understanding, chief among which is what I would call the art of negotiating across the various borders. This art is woven into the culture and its various expressions in daily life.

Today we need to affirm these sources and this art as hopes for a different world over against the dangerous view of a 'clash of civilizations' which has as its basis fear and insecurity, and as its goal the assertion of power. The well-publicized book by Samuel P. Huntington, despite some sprinkling of universalism, is basically a fundamentalist call to the West to arm itself against the onslaught of other civilizations, particularly the Islamic and the Asian.[16] In the process, the author espouses the view that the United States should defend its European cultural roots and should not give in to the dangers of multiculturalism. It is this set of ideas that are unfortunately being translated into the foreign and domestic policies of the empire. All this again forces us to look deep into the culture and ways of life of the subordinated peoples as guardians of peace, as they are also defenders of genuine universalism. At the grassroots level the common struggle for survival brings people together. The xenophobic discourses and irritations in the West regarding the legal status of foreigners, immigrants and refugees stand in stark contrast to the compassion and deep humanity with which simple people accept each other and help each other in daily life without regard to ethnic, religious or linguistic background.

IX. Conclusion

To what extent early Christianity as a movement of the marginalized was responsible for the decline of the Roman empire is a question to which probably no definite answer will ever be found. But one thing is clear: Christianity projected another set of values and ideals than those ones on which the empire relied – power, army, subjection and domination. The Christian movement of the marginalized of the time was also a powerful critique of the Roman empire, to which bestial and chaotic images are applied in the Book of Revelation. Monasteries with their 'blessed simplicity' and spirit of community embodied a utopian vision of the future and a different way of life.

The underdogs of history of today do not have the type of weapons required to challenge the might of the present empire and its military presence which polices all continents and seas; nor do they have the power to withstand globalization and the powers of transnational corporations and international monetary bodies. Instead they search for the sling of David. What they do have are their human ingenuity, resilience and their cultural weapons. To realize how much the local resources are able to project a different image of our world, we need to only pay attention to the worldwide environmental movement. It draws its inspiration and strategies from the local wisdom and resources to become a formidable force in our today's world.[17] This realization can only augment our hope.

The present situation of crisis and desperation has galvanized the victims to forge deep solidarity and pool together their local resources to resist the powers that be. In this struggle, one thing has been achieved quite decisively in the past couple of years, namely the pulling down of the ideological pillars on which the empire and globalization have been resting. The worldwide movement for a different world has exposed the hollowness of justification for domination, for war, for violence and for the inviolability of the market. We can only hope that it will not be long before the local torrents really turn into an inundation to submerge all that is inhuman in the present dominant order of the world. We also hope not only that a different world is possible, but that the twilight of this different world will appear soon on our horizons.

Notes

1. Fred Dallmayr, 'Empire or Cosmopolis? Civilization at the Crossroads', a paper presented at the international conference held at the University of Seville, Spain, on 'Neo-Colonialism in North-South Relations', 2–6 March 2004 . The jurist whose comment he is invoking is Francis Boyle, professor of international law at the University of Illinois.
2. Cf. Norman F. Cantor, *In the Wake of the Plague. The Black Death and the World It Made,* New York 2002.
3. Cf. Zygmunt Bauman, *Work, Consumerism and the New Poor,* Buckingham 1998.
4. Leon Trotsky, *The History of the Russian Revolution,* London ³1985.
5. Despite all my respect for the perceptive comments of the journalist Thomas Friedman on many issues of contemporary times, I find myself unable to share his view that the 'way forward' is to make globalization work for the poor. This contradicts the actual experience in the developing world, where it could signify efforts to fit a square into a round hole. Cf. Thomas Friedman, *The Lexus and the Olive Tree*, New York 2000. For a professionally critical perspective see the scholarly and insightful work by the Nobel Laureate for economics, Joseph Stiglitz, *Globalisation and Its Discontents,* London 2002.
6. Cf. Pierre Bourdieu, *Acts of Resistance. Against the Tyranny of the Market,* New York 1996.
7. Cf. Judith A. Berling, 'Threads of "Hope" in Traditional Chinese Religions', in Daniel L.Overmyer and Chi-Tim Lai (eds), *Interpretations of Hope in Chinese Religions and Christianity*, Hong Kong 2002, p. 8.
8. Cf. S.C.Malik (ed.), *Dissent, Protest and Reform in Indian Civilization*, Shimla 1997; Steven Parish, *Hierarchy and Its Discontents,* Delhi 1997.
9. James Scott, *Weapons of the Weak*, New Delhi 1990, pp.xvi – xvii. The author refers to the South East Asian practice of accepting kingship symbolically while resisting the king and the social order represented by him, and goes on to add: 'It goes without saying that these religious traditions in Southeast Asia have also formed the ideological basis for countless rebellions' (p.333). If we analyse the histories of independence struggles in many countries of the developing world, we will note how through the constant use of the 'weapons of the weak' the colonizers were led to the realization that the country could not be governed. Often the heroes of independence like Mahatma Gandhi, Sukarno or Kenyatta and others channelled the resistance of the ordinary people into large movements. Cf. Hira Singh, *Colonial Hegemony and Popular Resistance. Prince,*

Peasants and Paramount Power, Delhi 1998. See also the important series published in India with numerous case studies of resistance by tribals and other subordinated peoples: Ranajit Guha et al. (eds), *Subaltern Studies*, Delhi 1982 onwards.

10. Arundhati Roy, 'Confronting Empire', in *War Talk*, Cambridge, MA 2003, p. 112.
11. Nelson Mandela, *Long Walk to Freedom*, London 2003.
12. Isaiah Berlin, *Freedom and its Betrayal. Six Enemies of Human Liberty*, London 2003.
13. Dominique Lapierre, *A Thousand Suns*, Delhi 1999.
14. Cf. J.S. Grewal, 'Cleopatra's Nose', in Jayant V. Narlikar et al. (eds*), Philosophy of Science. Perspectives from Natural and Social Sciences*, Shimla 1992, pp. 188–98.
15. Cf. Martin Bernal, *Black Athena. The Afroasiatic Roots of Classical Civilization*, London 1991; also Anthony Disney and Emily Booth (eds), *Vasco da Gama and the Linking of Europe and Asia*, Delhi 2000.
16. Samuel P. Huntington, *The Clash of Civilizations and the Remaking of World Order*, New York and London 1996.
17. I cite here environmental movements like the 'Chipko movement' spearheaded by ordinary village women of India, or the overseeing of forest in eastern India by not less than 10,000 communities. They defend the forests against the predatory economic interests which want to fell the trees. Cf. Mark Poffenberger and Betsy McGean (eds), *Village Voices. Forest Choices. Joint Forest Management in India*, Delhi 1996.

Religion and Power: Towards the Political Sustainability of the World

RUDOLF VON SINNER

Introduction

The combination of religion and power gives at least a highly ambiguous, at most a highly explosive mixture. History is full of examples where religions have used power to dominate and have not refrained from destroying people they identified as enemies. Religious fanaticism is to be found in probably all religions, but it becomes most visible in the great world religions which sometimes assume power, together with a ruler or ruling class that belongs to them. In contrast, a positive notion of power has to be clearly distinguished from violence, as Hannah Arendt has pointed out so clearly.[1]

A relatively neutral definition of power comes from Plato, for whom *dynamis* is the effective force of every human being, and, moreover, the potency of every being to accomplish something. Max Weber's famous definition has it that 'power is every chance to carry through, within a social relationship, one's own will even against resistance'.[2] Paul Tillich insisted on the intrinsic relationship of power – as power of being which strives beyond itself – with love and justice.[3] In feminist and ecumenical circles empowerment has become a key term precisely for those who have, historically, been deprived of any power.[4] Power is a most complex 'thing' to define – and at the same time indispensable, as humans live together in never totally symmetrical relationships. Power is always power over somebody. Its legitimacy depends on whether it is used to serve a commonly agreed purpose.

In this modest contribution, I shall speak of power as *political* power, acknowledging its necessity and recognizing its ambiguity, and of empowerment of women and men as citizens as an important contribution of the churches, especially in societies which recently underwent a transition from an authoritarian to a democratic regime. I shall concentrate on Christian churches, as this is the form of religion I know best and is the main object of my research. However, it seems to me that the same aspects could be highlighted in other religions and comparable results be found. The use of power as inspired by the Triune God – and always bound to Godself – provides, as I shall argue, an important reference for empowering action under the present circumstances. Being the place where I live, work and research, Brazil will be the primary context of the following reflections, but glances on other countries will not be totally absent.

I. Political theology

Under the growing constraints of the ascending Nazi empire, Erik Peterson, a Lutheran theologian recently converted to Roman Catholicism, declared the end of any ' "political theology" which abuses Christian proclamation to legitimize a political situation'.[5] He saw the development of a trinitarian theology in the first four centuries of Christianity de-legitimizing the use of a monarchical imagery for God being reflected on earth by a human monarch, seeing 'One God, One Empire, One Emperor' in the same line. It was a thesis on the theological interpretation of the reign of Augustus under the sign of the birth of Christ, which Origen and especially Eusebius of Caesarea had used to exalt the Roman emperor and empire. However, Peterson's target was the religious legitimation of the German Reich under the Nazi ideology, which had been readily provided by both Roman Catholic and Protestant theologians at the time. He especially wanted to counter the 'political theology' of his friend Carl Schmitt, a professor of law, according to whom 'all important concepts of modern state doctrine are secularized theological concepts'[6] – as God is almighty, so the political sovereign holds all powers, including the power to call a state of emergency. For Peterson, a trinitarian God could not be reflected in human life, and so no state could claim to be God's image.

Some fifty years later, the 'new political theology' came into being, spearheaded by Johann Baptist Metz and Jürgen Moltmann. The latter took up explicitly the thesis defended by Peterson, but only in its critical stance against a monarchical political theology. According to Moltmann, the doctrine of the Trinity did not put an end to any political theology, but provided the ground for a democratic notion of politics, de-legitimizing any monopolisation of power.[7] Leonardo Boff took a similar line a few years later, seeing the Trinity as a critique of the accumulation of power in politics and in the church as experienced in the Brazilian context and 'as a model for any just, egalitarian (while respecting differences) social organization', postulating 'a society that can be the image and likeness of the Trinity'.[8]

Both this new type of political theology and Latin American liberation theology have made it clear that there is no such thing as a political neutrality of the church. The church is either on the side of those in power or on the side of those without power, or in a dialectical position between the two. The basis for this position is both a particular belief in God and a particular reading of the context. We should beware of easy analogies, as if the image of God were readily deducible from human reality – as Feuerbach thought – or we could easily deduce a particular form of society from our image of God. Rather, our image of God derives from a complex interaction between text and context, gospel and culture. However, Moltmann, Boff and others are right in insisting that a God who is three persons-in-relation, who manifests Godself in diverse forms but maintains the same identity, who is loving and dynamic rather than a distant ruler, has much to tell to human persons who are deprived of their rights and lack even the most basic items for survival, longing for respect and a decent living. This is not to say that a strictly monotheistic image of God could not resist the abuse of power and incite its correct use – on the contrary, it was precisely Israel which dissociated rule and salvation, in a different way from Egypt, and thus demythologized the king, depriving him of any divine character.[9] But in a Christian context it is most meaningful to explore the trinitarian image to think about life in the household of God.[10]

II. A new task in a changed context

Political theology, as I understand it here, is an explicit theological reflection on the political positioning of the church within a given context. Liberation theology is such a political theology, inasmuch as it forged resistance against political and economic domination.[11] Under the military regimes in Latin America, Christian base communities, inspired by a liberating theology, provided a basis both for resistance against the state's repression and for the struggle to improve everyday life – the conquest of power and water supply, proper sewerage, schooling and leisure facilities and the like. Especially in Brazil, they received the backing of the Roman Catholic hierarchy. In South Africa, resistance went against the racist system of apartheid, backed both by the local churches and by international church bodies like the World Council of Churches. Those churches which continued to defend apartheid as a system of racial separation willed by God were discredited by the Reformed World Alliance and their membership suspended. In South Korea, *minjung* theology assembled 'the people' for resistance under dictatorship. In these and many other cases churches were, in differing degrees, both part of the problem – inasmuch as they supported the regime – and provided important, sometimes unique spaces of opposition.

Thankfully, in all the countries cited – and, indeed, in many others – the political situation has changed radically. A transition from an authoritarian regime to democracy has taken place, and organizations of civil society have been (re-)admitted. This has meant on the one hand a loss of influence on the side of the churches. They are no longer the most prominent, let alone the only, space for critical political activity. At best they are one among many agents of civil society. On the other hand, a new stance in a political theology is needed for this new situation. What Walter Altmann, taking up a concept developed by Ulrich Duchrow, has named a 'critical-constructive participation' of the churches in politics, is now no longer possible only in 'old', Western democracies, but has become a real option in post-transition countries.[12] Liberation theology, as it makes its 'option for the poor' and strives to liberate from all oppression based on social, economic, gender, ethnic or other hierarchies, has to leave mere opposition and contribute actively towards the well-being of society – not rarely being in a position of considerable political power, as a member of the government or government-related agencies, the leader of a powerful NGO or even as a church leader. In an influential article, the Brazilian Hugo Assmann called for a 'Theology of Solidarity and Citizenship' as the continuation of liberation theology.[13] At the dawn of a post-apartheid society in South Africa, Charles Villa-Vicencio claimed a 'post-exilic theology as a theology of reconstruction and nation-building'. He states that:

> Utopian dreams are important, but not enough to create something that is qualitatively different from the structures of oppression . . . For the dreams of the oppressed to become a reality they are to be translated into political programmes and law-making that benefit those who have longed for, and fought for, the new age, while protecting the new society against the abuses which marked past oppression. This ultimately is what a liberatory theology of reconstruction is all about.[14]

This is not an entirely new position. Theologies of nation-building were developed in Europe, India and in the broad ecumenical debate since before World War II, giving birth to the Life and Work movement.[15] However, they have assumed varied importance in different times and places, presupposing a moment of 'awakening' after a deep crisis or devastating disaster which is to be overcome through a democratic process to which a variety of agents are invited to contribute.

In my reading, the time of 'big phrases', be they in favour of a glorious utopia or simply opposing a reigning power, qualified as evil, is over. Certainly the need for hope, fuelled by a vision of what is to come, continues, and a critical identification of oppressing powers is still important. However, it is urgent to contribute to changes that make a concrete difference to people's lives, empowering them to be bold citizens, conscious of their place in society with the right to full participation and the possibility to effectively exercise it. One way to understand this process is the construction of *cidadania* (citizenship), to which I shall now turn.[16] We find similar struggles in other countries.

III. The churches as schools for citizenship

Citizenship means the belonging of a person to a particular state, implying certain rights and duties. Beyond this technical definition, it has become customary to use the term to denote the effective access to and exercise of these rights and duties by citizens. In a more ample sense, as has become customary in today's Brazil, it can also be seen as the subjective side of democracy. If the latter is a system of government formally guaranteed by a set of representative institutions subject to a regular and competitive vote, and through legal texts that describe its basic purposes and the rules for its functioning, *cidadania* means the actual participation of citizens in democracy, being conscious of their citizenship and striving to exercise their rights and duties.

This, of course, presupposes that citizens know about their rights and duties. Moreover, it is necessary that people believe that their abiding by such rights and duties as foreseen by law is actually doing them some good. It is precisely this aspect which cannot simply be taken for granted. In Brazil, for instance, democracy brought excellent law texts, but old power structures have remained, as has a widespread distrust in the functioning of the public apparatus. There are good historical reasons for such lack of trust. Law was corrupted during the military regime, although formal legality continued in many aspects throughout the authoritarian phase. Even after the return to democracy, many citizens experience a difficulty in exercising their rights unless they have a 'godfather' in the right place at the right time. According to the Brazilian anthropologist Roberto DaMatta, there are two cultural systems operating at the same time.[17] The traditional one interprets human beings as 'persons' related to a particular 'family' headed by the father: an entrepreneur, a politician or another powerful patron. It is through their relationship with such a patron that persons receive what they need, unlike others who do not have such protection. On the other hand, the law is based on 'individuals' with equality. These, however, are regarded as inferior, as the saying goes: 'for the friends, everything, for the enemies, the law'. That is, the 'individuals' who depend on the law have no friends and are, effectively, excluded from 'real' society because they do not belong to a 'family'. While providing some form of integration and advantages, family-type relationships are an obstacle to the recognition of equality and difference of the individual, as well as to a more general and universal reliance on commonly agreed rules which are crucial for a democracy that is worthy of its name.

The churches do play an important role in the formation of citizens, both because of their influence on moral behaviour and because they reach a considerable part of the population, even in very poor areas. It seems that the most effective there are those who least speak about *cidadania* and the conquest of rights: the so-called *crentes* (believers), mainly Pentecostals. To cite a concrete area where their relevance becomes most obvious, let me cite the omnipresent crime, especially around drug trafficking. The author of the book on which the much-praised film *Cidade de Deus* (City of God) was based, Paulo Lins, during his anthropological studies wrote an article, together with a colleague, on 'Bandits and Evangelicals'. In it he argued that 'the myth that the way into banditism does not have any way out meets its safe exception in their conversion to the gospel'.[18] Similarly, Drauzio Varella, who served for some time as a doctor to the enormous São Paulo Carandiru prison, said that the Assemblies of God represented, most probably, the only real project of re-socialization in the prison.[19] This is because those who convert in prison are exempted from the rigid law imposed by the inmates and gain respect and protection. Moreover, they might find a stable network of relationships when they leave the penitentiary, which can help them into a non-criminal life. This is precisely what this church itself claims: it restores lives in transforming women and men from the margins of society, who become visibly 'decent and honourable' persons.[20]

This might sound utterly moralistic and distant from real *cidadania*. Indeed, the basis for the church's positioning over against the state is clearly based on Romans 13: 'Let every person be subject to the governing authorities . . .', although a small window for critique is opened through Acts 5.29: 'We must obey God rather than any human authority.' The

Assemblies of God insist much more on duties than on rights. Nevertheless, this church does restore a feeling of dignity to women and men, so that they may perceive themselves as true citizens. They are empowered to live their lives as respectable subjects.

The rapid growth of Pentecostal churches in Brazil, as in other countries of Latin America, Africa and Asia, shows that they have also become a political force. In many places, they are courted by politicians to gain their votes.[21] Obviously, empowerment here easily mutates into power politics with all its ambiguities, not seldom sliding into corporativism and, worse, into corruption. But this should not lead us to overlook the important benefits these churches provide for their faithful, apparently in ways more effective than those adopted by the Christian base communities.[22]

What I want to underline here is that, to be consolidated, a democracy needs citizens with a positive – not positivistic – notion of law and a basic trust in each other.[23] This is crucial for a sound balance of power in public space. Churches and, more broadly speaking, religions can both provide a critical-constructive partnership with the authorities and be a school for democracy. Of course, their own organization cannot be exempted from the challenge of *cidadania*; otherwise they would lose their credibility. Luther was right in insisting on church and state as two different kingdoms, in the sense that their realms and specific responsibilities must not be blurred. However, he also insisted that both kingdoms come under God's judgment, and that the church has the duty to be a guardian of the state's realm. Romans 13 has to be read together with Revelation 13, clearly showing the ambivalence of public authority. We should not, however, forget that often it was the churches which accumulated and misused their power, and that, historically, human rights had to be gained against rather than with the churches' will and power. Churches do not have something to offer because of their own perfection, but because their power – and, indeed, their notion of power – is intrinsically bound to God's power, in which it finds its most profound inspiration and its most severe critique. Their trust is grounded in God, from where it can be expanded to other people, offering insights for an ethics of vulnerability rather than violence.[24]

IV. Conclusion: religion, power and sustainability

Power is highly ambiguous, as I remarked earlier, but it is indispensable. Political power – sometimes combined with, sometimes against, religious power – affects everybody. It is not helpful to see it in a merely negative, demonizing way. If that happens there are only two options: move to a remote 'island' or build up cells of resistance, thus missing the chance of a constructive co-operation, which I believe is what is most needed today. Power should be seen as a necessity, the quality of which is to be constantly controlled by, ideally, the whole population. For it to be sustainable, healthy for humans and for the natural environment, it needs the critical-constructive collaboration of all.

To this end, from a Christian standpoint, theological references are needed for measuring the quality of the power exercised. Much is to be found in the Bible, which can ground a sound notion of power; Hans–Ruedi Weber made it even a focus for a biblical theology.[25] In a Christian perspective, human power is always bound to God's power, which empowers human beings to be co-creators, but limits their exercise of power through values like love and justice. Whosoever wants to exercise power should first and foremost serve. Then there is the central fact that Christ humbled himself by becoming human, using his divine power to heal and empower people, especially those on the margins. The paradigm of power is God who becomes human and forgoes his power. God is a dynamic (sic!) and compassionate God, diverse in Godself as a community of persons-in-loving-relationship. On the basis of this trinitarian image of God, Christians can make an important contribution to the sustainability of the world, continuing a liberative theology through a theology of *cidadania*.

Notes

1. Hannah Arendt, *On Violence*, New York 1970.
2. Max Weber, *Wirtschaft und Gesellschaft* (1922), Tübingen ⁵1972, p. 28; cf. Volker Gerhardt, 'Macht I. Philosophisch', in *Theologische Realenzyklopädie*, vol. 21, Berlin 2000, pp. 648–52.
3. Paul Tillich, *Love, Power and Justice. Ontological Analysis and Ethical Application*, New York 1954.
4. Cf. Charles C. West, 'Power', in Nicholas Lossky et al. (eds.), *Dictionary of the Ecumenical Movement*, Geneva ²2002, pp. 919–23.
5. Erik Peterson, 'Der Monotheismus als politisches Problem: Ein Beitrag zur Geschichte der politischen Theologie im Imperium Romanum' (1935), in *Theologische Traktate. Ausgewählte Schriften* Vol. 1, Würzburg 1994, pp. 23–81: 59. For a wider view on the issue at stake, see the very instructive work by David Nicholls, *Deity and Domination. Images of God and the State in the Nineteenth and Twentieth Centuries* (1989), London and New York 1994.
6. Carl Schmitt, *Politische Theologie. Vier Kapitel von der Souveränität* (1922), Berlin ⁶1993, p. 43 (ET *Political Theology*, Cambridge, MA 1985).

7. Jürgen Moltmann, *The Trinity and the Kingdom of God*, London and New York 1981.

8. Leonardo Boff, *Trinity and Society*, London 1988, p. 11; cf. Rudolf von Sinner, *Reden vom dreieinigen Gott in Brasilien und Indien. Grundzüge einer ökumenischen Hermeneutik im Dialog mit Leonardo Boff und Raimon Panikkar*, Tübingen 2003, pp. 59–195. Cf. also Boff's famous book on *Church, Charism and Power. Liberation Theology and the Institutional Church* (1981), New York and London 1986.

9. Cf. Jan Assmann, *Herrschaft und Heil. Politische Theologie in Altägypten, Israel und Europa*, Munich and Vienna 2000.

10. Cf. Konrad Raiser, *Ecumenism in Transition. A Paradigm Shift in the Ecumenical Movement?*, Geneva 1991, who describes an apparent shift from a christocentric to a trinitarian theology in the ecumenical movement. For more recent reflections, among others on the legitimate use of power in a globalized world, see his *For a Culture of Life. Transforming Globalization and Violence*, Geneva 2002, and 'Rationale for a New Ecumenical Discourse on Power', outline of a paper presented to the Consultation on 'Interrogating and Redefining Power', Crê-Bérard, Switzerland, 10 December 2003, kindly sent to me by the author on my request. Raiser ends with the phrase: 'There is no better way to liberate ourselves from the capitalist or militarist models of power than to return to the trinitarian model.'

11. For an already 'classical' theoretical reflection on liberation theology as a theology of the political, see Clodovis Boff, *Theology and Praxis*, Maryknoll, NY 1987. What is meant here by 'political theology' is also called 'public theology' in other contexts and by other authors; cf. Peter Scott and William T. Cavanaugh (eds.), *The Blackwell Companion to Political Theology*, Oxford 2004.

12. Walter Altmann, *Luther and Liberation. A Latin American Perspective* (1992), Eugene, OR 2000, pp. 69–83, esp. 8off.; Ulrich Duchrow (ed.), *Lutheran Churches – Salt or Mirror of Society*, Geneva 1977, pp. 300–7.

13. Hugo Assmann, *Crítica à Lógica da Exclusão. Ensaios sobre economia e teologia*, São Paulo 1994, pp. 13–36.

14. Charles Villa-Vicencio, *A Theology of Reconstruction. Nation-building and Human Rights*, Cambridge 1992, p. 29.

15. Paul Abrecht, 'Society', in Nicholas Lossky et al. (eds.), *Dictionary of the Ecumenical Movement* (n.4), pp. 1049–53; see also Lewis S. Mudge and Thomas Wieser (eds.), *Democratic Contracts for Sustainable and Caring Societies. What Can Churches and Christian Communities Do?*, Geneva 2000.

16. Cf. Rudolf von Sinner, 'Healing Relationships in Society. The Struggle for Citizenship in Brazil', *International Review of Mission*, 93, 2004, no. 369, pp. 238–54. In what follows, I am taking up elements of this article freely.

17. Roberto DaMatta, *Carnivals, Rogues, and Heroes: An Interpretation of the Brazilian Dilemma*, Notre Dame, IN 1991; David J. Hess and Roberto A.

DaMatta (eds.), *The Brazilian Puzzle. Culture on the Borderlands of the Western World*, New York 1995.

18. Paulo Lins and Maria de Lourdes da Silva, 'Bandidos e Evangélicos: Extremos que se Tocam', *Religião e Sociedade* 15, 1990, no. 1, p. 172.
19. Drauzio Varella, *Estação Carandiru*, São Paulo 1999.
20. Cf. Cecília Mariz, *Coping with Poverty. Pentecostals and Christian Base Communities in Brazil*, Philadelphia 1994.
21. Cf. Paul Freston, *Evangelicals and Politics in Asia, Africa and Latin America*, Oxford 2001; Edward L. Cleary and Hannah W. Stewart-Gambino, *Power, Politics and Pentecostals in Latin America*, Boulder, CO 1998.
22. Cf. John Burdick, *Looking for God in Brazil. The Progressive Catholic Church in Urban Brazil's Religious Arena*, Berkeley, CA 1993.
23. Cf. Mark E. Warren (ed.). *Democracy and Trust*, Cambridge 1999.
24. Cf. Sturla J. Stålsett, *Trust in the Market? Social Capital and the Ethics of Vulnerability*, 2003, http://www.iadb.org/etica/ingles/index-i.cfm; Rudolf von Sinner, 'Confiança e convivência. Aportes para uma hermenêutica da confiança na convivência humana', *Estudos Teológicos* 44, 2004, no. 1, pp. 127–43.
25. Hans-Ruedi Weber, *Power. Focus for a Biblical Theology*, Geneva 1989.

Economics and Spirituality: Towards a More Just and Sustainable World

JUNG MO SUNG

I. A different economic system is both possible and necessary

On principle, we always can and should state that a different world and a different economic system are possible. We can state this since it is a historical and social fact to the extent that all societies and economies, like all human institutions, are historically situated and have a beginning and an end. But besides its being a factual statement, we *should* always state that a different world is possible, since not to do so means absolutizing the ruling system. And social systems that are treated as or stated to be absolute – 'There is no alternative' – become idols and always require sacrifice of human lives.

The duty of proclaiming and fighting for a different world stems not only from this philosophical or theological position of denying the absolute character of the present world but mainly from the grave social crises – poverty, structural unemployment, social exclusion, violence, and the like – and the environmental crisis brought about by the present model of economic globalization. The present economic-social system is both unjust and unsustainable.

It is unsustainable because the economic growth of the present globalization model needs the pattern of consumption of the wealthy nations to be introduced increasingly into the rest of the world, levelling up life styles and consumer desires. It is this levelling up of consumer patterns and social relationships that allows world-scale production and a world consumer market, without which the great transnational corporations would lose their competitive advantage. This expansion is legitimized by the myth of economic progress, which states that there are no limits to economic growth, that this growth can and should be imitated by the whole world, and that there is a harmony between technical progress, economic growth and human development. In other words, the more economic growth and the more consumption there are, the more human development and achievement there are also.

This central and foundational myth of the modern world is present not only in books and speeches but also in the daily lives of those immersed in these economics and this culture. Let us take as an example the deposition of a former director of Coca Cola, Brazil, Marilene Pereira Lopes, then fifty-one years old: 'On the night of 17 May 2001 I went to sleep thinking of the heavy workload I had to face the next day. When I woke up I had no sensation in my left arm. . . . In the early morning I had suffered a stroke in the left side of my brain. . . . People believe that if things are going well at work, that if you are climbing the ladder of professional life, everything else will be all right. I had to go through a drama to realize that this is not true. I soon recovered my speech, though with difficulty. I resolved to submit my resignation and to change my way of life.'[1]

Not only does the human body have its limits: nature itself has limits that do not permit the consumption levels of the wealthy nations to be spread worldwide. In fact, this obsession with increasing economic growth and consumption is one of the chief causes of the environmental crisis. Besides this, the upper and middle classes in the poor countries can succeed in fulfilling their desire to imitate the consumer patterns of the wealthy nations only by increasing the burden of exploitation of the poorest and by reducing social spending, thereby generating a division within the country between those included in this new global market and those excluded from it.[2] To the extent that the pressure of the global capitalist economy and the desires to imitate its pattern of consumption push economic and social processes in this direction of levelling up consumer spending and the frenetic quest for higher consumption, so social and environmental crises become worse.

Faced with these crises, many capitalist ideologies obviously spring up to proclaim that the continued advance of science and technology will be capable of overcoming the limitations of nature and that the free market will prove able to surmount these social crises. They proclaim a blind faith in science, in technology and in the market in an attempt to hide or divert attention from the suffering of billions of people and the destruction of our environment. The deaths of entire species and of millions of human beings will be the sacrifices needed if economic growth is to make the realization of the wish for unlimited consumption possible.

To sum up, the present capitalist economic system is not only unjust but is also economically, socially and environmentally unsustainable. Faced with this situation, theology and religious groups have to contribute from the specific viewpoint of theology and religion. This means that we both can and must contribute by criticizing the absolutization of the capitalist market, the idolatry of the market and the myth of human progress, which demand and justify sacrifices of human lives and of the environment; we must also criticize that obsessive desire for consumption stemming from the illusion that imitating the consumption patterns of the wealthy elite will turn us into better human beings.

II. Utopia and possible world

The ethical and prophetic duty of denouncing oppressions and injustices and proclaiming a different world derives also from our desire to live in a more just world, better for all of us. However, we must be clear that not all the worlds we desire are possible. That is, desiring a different world does not mean that it can become possible through the mere fact of our desiring it, since human beings are capable of desiring things that are beyond the bounds of possibility. Nevertheless, utopias – those imaginings of a 'perfect', though impossible, world – are necessary if we are to retain a standpoint from which we are able to criticize the present world and which makes it possible for us to devise alternative plans for society.

However much we may wish our utopian dream to be fulfilled, we need to have the historical realism to perceive the limits of the human condition and of the natural world and to struggle for historically achievable goals. Those who struggle to realize impossible desires commit errors that prevent them from constructing viable alternatives.[3] This recognition of the limits of history and of the human condition is not something we find easy, since it implies divesting ourselves of our finest dreams of a world freed from all injustice and oppression, a world without victims. The existence of victims is the point of departure for all prophecy and the criterion for critique of all social norms and systems, and, as Enrique Dussel has written, 'Victims are inevitable. Their inevitability derives from the fact that is empirically *impossible* for a norm, act, institution, or system of ethics *to be perfect* in their expression and consequences. A perfect system is *empirically impossible*.'[4] This impossibility derives from the fact that we cannot perfectly and fully know all the factors that make up nature and social life, nor do we possess the infinite energy needed to manage the system perfectly. Since victims are inevitable, prophetic action is and always will be necessary.

Some Christians may have recourse to the exodus narrative to situate their hope of liberation of the poor and of all the oppressed within the course of history. However, we should not lose sight of the fact that the exodus did not mean the end of victims in the history of Israel, and that faith in the resurrection of Jesus, the Messiah defeated and killed on a cross, led the first Christian communities to realize that the kingdom of God is not fully brought about in history, that we can see it only in anticipatory signs.

III. Economic, social and environmental sustainability

For a different world we desire to become possible, this new society has to be economically, socially and environmentally sustainable. Its economic system has to be capable of producing more than the minimum limit of the basic needs of the whole population and of replacing means of production as they wear out, besides making the necessary investments to meet the needs of new generations. An economic system that is amenable, just and free, but incapable of satisfying these minimum conditions will not survive for long. Furthermore, the various production processes have to be related to one another and to form a system. In other words, there has to be a system for coordinating the social division of work that is efficient in linking the innumerable factors and processes of which it is composed. An example would be the linking of production of basic goods with natural resources and existing technologies, with the organization of productive units (as private, community or state enterprises, or as cooperatives, and so on), and with people's needs and desires. We need a system that responds, with efficiency and with social justice, to the question: what to produce, how much, how, and with whom. In the present capitalist model the market is the main and virtually the sole coordinator, which is proving unjust and unsustainable, while in the Soviet socialist model the coordinator was central planning, which proved to be inefficient. We still do not know precisely what the new type of coordination of the social division of work should be, but it should probably be a linkage of the market, government regulation (plans setting economic and social targets), and actions by civil society (such as campaigns by environmentalists, NGOs, consumer rights groups and the like).

A society can reproduce itself satisfactorily only to the extent that its social relationships and institutions are also sustainable. That is, the manner in which it is organized has to keep the social fabric intact. To do this, the production, distribution and consumption of economic goods has to pay sufficient attention to the needs and wishes of the population, or at least of a major part of it. There must also be a cultural convergence and a spirituality that transforms a multitude of individuals into a society in which each individual feels a participant in or member of it. Besides this, a relatively stable society is not possible without the existence of symbols, rites and myths that attract and bring together the erratic desires of individuals. In present-day capitalism, the main agent for bringing these desires together is the market – especially through advertising and the mass media – which reduces or directs almost all desires to the desire for consumption and for commercial goods.

Economic and social sustainability are interdependent and equally tied to environmental sustainability. Living beings keep themselves alive to the degree that they integrate with their environment and draw the elements necessary for their survival from it. In this interaction the sum total of living beings modifies the environment, which leads them also to modify their manner of interaction with it. Environmental problems arise when a 'natural' disaster occurs – such as the impact of a large meteorite – or when one species, such as the human species, acquires the capacity to destroy the environment. And to destroy one's environment is to commit suicide. To take natural resources from the environment at a rate greater than its capacity for regeneration is to compromise our possibility of survival, especially that of future generations. And the present rush to deplete natural resources comes, very largely, from the obsession with greater consumption.

IV. Sustainable development and human needs

In the struggle to create a more just and sustainable society in social and environmental terms, the theme of satisfying the basic needs of the poor holds a central place. No society can be considered just and socially sustainable if a major part of its population is unable to satisfy its basic needs. However, the definition of what constitutes a need is not so simple. To analyse the matter, let us take a text from the World Commission on Environment and Development:

> To satisfy human needs and aspirations is the principal aim of development. [. . .] For there to be sustainable development, it is necessary for all to have their basic needs met and for them to be granted opportunities for realizing their aspirations to a better life.
>
> Standards of living that are above the basic minimum are sustainable only if the general patterns of consumption are aimed at achieving sustainable development in the long term. Even so, many of us live beyond the world's ecological means, as shown by the use of energy, for

example. Needs are determined socially or culturally, and sustainable development requires the promotion of values that keep consumption levels within ecological limits and to what everyone, in a reasonable fashion, can aspire.[5]

This text provides us with two notions of need: (a) basic needs understood as the minimum required for the continuance of bodily life, such as a minimum number of calories, a dwelling, health – the standard most generally adopted by social movements and churches involved in satisfying the basic needs of everyone; (b) socially and culturally determined needs.

In the first notion of need, that of the minimum needed for the continuance of bodily life, we are presented with an image of human beings faced with their organic needs without taking their social relationships and the cultural aspects of their lives into consideration. In the second, human beings are seen as beings in relation to others in such a way that their own needs are no longer determined by their bodies but by the culture and social relationships in which they live. Now the text says, correctly, that the aim of development is, or ought to be, meeting the needs of all people and giving them the opportunity of realizing their human aspirations. In this case, development cannot satisfy merely our physiological needs, since we are basically social and cultural beings, and it is within a culture that we can express and try to realize our aspirations. Furthermore, the problem of sustainability arises only in reference to the needs determined by the culture, since these are needs beyond the basic minimum level for survival and so can create social and environmental problems.

We are beings that need, besides these basic material goods, to be accepted by other people and to belong to a social group. The desire to be accepted as a person and to belong to a particular group is almost as vital for us as food and drink. Clearly the satisfaction of bodily needs, such as hunger and thirst, is the condition *sine qua non* for people to remain alive and so able to go on wishing for acceptance and to belong to a community. Nevertheless, if people lose the desire to live because they feel totally rejected by everyone else and not to belong to a group, even to a 'virtual' community, they no longer have need of food and drink, since what they now want is to die.

The relationship between physiological or organic needs, culturally determined needs and personal desires is a non-linear and complex one. That is, there is no relationship of linear hierarchy between them, in which organic needs would be at the bottom, with culturally determined needs coming just above them, and finally personal desires at the top. We are motivated or attracted by our desires, and it is in the pursuit of their fulfilment that we need to satisfy our organic and cultural needs.

In our consumer culture, recognition by a particular social group requires reaching the level of consumption desired and demanded by that group. As students of contemporary culture say, our identity is intimately linked to our pattern of consumption: 'Tell me what you consume, and I shall tell you who you are.' The higher the level of consumption, the greater the possession of 'being' – the reason why people spend hundreds of thousands of dollars on a car, or $35,000 on a bottle of scent. And many of the non-rich or poor feel themselves less than human because they do not satisfy the cultural necessity of consuming certain products or famous brands. The rich seek to consume ever more to mark themselves out as 'superior', the middle classes and the poor try to imitate the level of consumption of the class above them, and social and environmental crises become more and more acute.

Without different cultural and spiritual values, without different desires that will modify current culturally and socially determined needs, a different world with a more just and human sustainable development is not possible.

V. Spirituality and the human condition

If we are to overcome the crisis of the present world and build ourselves a different, sustainable and more just world, people will have to adopt a notion of sustainability and make it part of their daily life and of the way they tackle their desires. The notion of sustainability implies that of limitation, in terms of both the human condition and the social and environmental fabric, and it also implies the impossibility of constructing a social order in which we shall all live in perfect harmony with nature and among ourselves. That is, the notion of sustainability implies that we shall be able to have a better world only if we turn away from the project of building a 'perfect' one.

This is a very important spiritual and social paradox: we can only make ourselves better people if we admit that we shall never be truly saints or perfect human beings. It is the existential acceptance of our condition as ambiguous beings that makes us better. This is the reason why forgiveness, mercy and compassion are central elements in gospel spirituality. In the same way, we can build a better and sustainable world only if we assume that we cannot build any world of completeness, be it of unlimited consumption, perfect justice, or perfect harmony between us and nature.

This is the only way we can overcome the central and foundational myth of modernity: that the progress of science and of human beings will lead us to a full and perfect world. This myth is, ultimately, a rebellion against the human condition. It is the expression of a desire that we human beings should become the builders of a world free from the ambiguities of our human condition, even of death itself. The present myths surrounding the future of genetic engineering, for example, are nothing more than expressions of this rebellion and of the desire to turn ourselves into post-human beings.

When we propose or simply desire the formation of a world without victims or conflicts, we are, basically, sharing the same bases and illusions of this myth of modernity. And from within these illusions there is no historical possibility of a sustainable and more just world.

I believe that a true break with the founding myths of modernity cannot come from simply rebelling against capitalism. We need to have a true 'spiritual revolution'. We have to abandon a spirituality – religious or secular – that seeks to outgrow the human condition into a supra-human situation, one of fullness and absolute security, in favour of a spirituality lived as a way that leads us to discover our human condition and be reconciled with it. This spirituality both allows us to share and is found through our sharing in the sufferings, fears and insecurities of other individuals and groups (compassion), and also in their hopes, struggles and joys (solidarity). Without this encounter with persons who are suffering, without the encounters found in compassion and in struggles together, there can be no encounter with oneself or with the Spirit who breathes over us, and without these encounters there can be no reconciliation.

I also believe that Christian communities and those of other religions can and must contribute to the gestation of this spiritual revolution. They *can* because spirituality is the specific subject of religions in the modern world; they *must* because, if they do not do so, other similar groups will not be able to proceed with this fundamental task in the gestation of a different world. Without spiritual revolution there will be no real economic revolution, since capitalism is, in fact, an economic system based on and motivated by deep spiritual beliefs, and consumerism is a form of religious expression in our daily lives.

A different, more just, and sustainable world will become a reality only if a significant part of society takes this spirituality upon itself and becomes capable of leading many others to wish to take part in the building of this different world.

Translated by Paul Burns

Notes

1. 'A vida além dos limites' in *Exame* (São Paulo), 16 April 2004. This is the main Brazilian journal aimed at business executives.

2. On this desire to imitate the consumption of the elite, social problems and theology see, e.g., J. M. Sung, *Desejo, Mercado e religião*, Petrópolis 1998.

3. On this important and difficult topic, see, e.g., F. Hinkelammert, *La crítica de la razón utópica*, San José, Costa Rica 1998; J. M. Sung, *Sujeito e sociedades complexas: para repensar os horizontes utópicos*, Petrópolis 2002.

4. E. Dussel, *Ética da libertação na idade da globalização e da exclusão*, Petrópolis 2000, p. 373.

5. World Commission on Environment and Development, *Our Common Future*, 2a, 1987 (here Portuguese translation 1991, pp. 46–7).

War and Paths to Peace in the Palestine-Israel Conflict

SERGIO NICOLÁS YAHNI

In memory of Dr Thabeth Thabeth, a Palestinian activist
assassinated by the Israeli army at the start of the intifada

In April 2002, in the company of a group of Israeli activists, I visited the city of Ramallah, after I had just spent twenty-eight days in a military prison for refusing to serve in the Israeli army of occupation. The tanks of the army in which I had refused to serve were to be seen on every corner, and the destruction they had left behind them was equally in evidence.

There were seven of us. We made our way in surreptitiously, avoiding the military checkpoints. Our objective was to get into the *Muqata'*, the head-quarters of the Palestinian police in the city, where the Palestinian president and his closest associates were being besieged. Together with the Palestinian authorities were a number of foreign activists, who acted as a protective shield. We wanted to be there, next to the besieged leaders, part of the international show of solidarity, protesting against the re-occupation of the city by Israeli troops, raising our voices for peace and against the occupation.

We had spent the night before our attempt to penetrate the Israeli security cordon around the *Muqata'* in a Palestinian hospital, next to those wounded in the last month of battle. The hospital management had converted the car park into a mass grave, since there was no more room in the refrigeration chambers of the morgue. We had never expected to be well received in Ramallah, still less did we expect to be greeted with warmth and friendship in a Palestinian hospital besieged by army tanks and in which most of the inmates had been seriously wounded by this same army. But we managed to spend the night talking and discussing with wounded Palestinians, sharing cups of coffee. Some of the Palestinians had been combatants. One told how the ambulance that was bringing him to hospital had been intercepted by soldiers, who had taken him to a military interrogation centre and then left him outside in the rain. The military doctor in attendance had been concerned only with whether he was able to continue with the interrogation, making no attempt to give him any sort of treatment. Another of the wounded asked us about how people were doing in Israel, what they thought of Sharon. Previously, at the start of the uprising, he had been a construction worker in Tel Aviv. Now he had been out of work for over a year.

For all of us who were there, that night was a re-encounter with the possibility that this war, which has in effect lasted for almost a hundred years, might have an end, a re-encounter with the possibility that Israelis and Palestinians might partake in and share out this land that has witnessed so many deaths. This was our window of opportunity, opened after seven years of negotiations between Israel and the Palestinian Authority, which ended in an unnecessary bloodletting. We, though, were a handful of dreamers declaring that Israelis and Palestinians could share the future, that a future without wars is possible, that it is within our grasp.

On the other hand, even if peace can be built through dialogue, it is governments who can and must create the conditions to make dialogue possible.

I. Peace and reconciliation: the logical outlook and the Palestine-Israel reality

There are no *de luxe* wars. War is a feud of death and crime. Even if people talk of just wars – such as the war against Nazi Germany, for example – however just a particular war may be, war makes people commit atrocities that condemn populations to extreme suffering. In World War II, for example, the bombing and destruction of the city of Dresden by the Allies had no military objective. Dresden was bombed out of revenge and caused totally unnecessary suffering on the part of its non-combatant inhabitants.

We need to bear this in mind when we speak of reconciliation, that is, when we try to move beyond the military aspect of the end of the conflict, the ceasefire, and the political-governmental aspect, a peace agreement. Reconciliation belongs to civil society and has to do with healing the wounds opened by violence.

The ending of a conflict has three essential phases. The first is the ceasefire, which makes the use of arms give way to the negotiation table and means that parties to the conflict engage themselves to forbid the use of force as long as negotiations continue. This phase should include conditions to allow effective development of negotiations, such as – among other things, the freeing of prisoners of war in an international conflict, or of political detainees in the case of a conflict within a single state, the partial or total withdrawal of troops or, in the case of an internal conflict, political measures that allow the opposition to express itself freely and not through use of arms, and forms of verifying the development of the process in itself and the application of agreements reached.

The second phase is a political agreement between the parties: a peace agreement, which can come only from a ceasefire. In this phase the parties agree the future relationship between them, allocation of territory, economic and political relationships, and the means of negotiating future conflicts. Or the internal political structures within a state that will allow both sides to express themselves freely and solve internal crises by peaceful means.

Finally, we can speak of a reconciliation phase. Reconciliation between the parties to a conflict has the aim of allowing the resolution of the problems that led to hostilities by healing the wounds created during the conflict and making reparation for the crimes committed during the hostilities by creating institutions that convince the parties to the conflict that the end of the conflict has brought justice with it.

From an institutional point of view these three phases have to be consecutive and cannot be jumbled together. Neither can conditions for reconciliation be created without the parties to the conflict and their victims believing that justice has been done in making reparation for the crimes. At the same time a peace process, even if it is a political process, cannot advance without the active intervention of civil society. It is civil society that has to exert pressure for a non-violent solution to the conflict, it is the interests of civil society that must prevail in the political negotiations in a peace process, and finally reconciliation is not between political bodies but between civilian bodies and individuals on both sides of the conflict.

This was the 'route map' that brought about the end of apartheid in South Africa. First the ANC was made legal and political prisoners, including, of course, Nelson Mandela, were set free. This process provided space for negotiations that culminated in an electoral process. The general elections in South Africa not only erased *apartheid* from the political future of the country but created conditions for reconciliation among the parties, a process led by Archbishop Desmond Tutu. In the South African process, parallel to the institutional development of relations between the government and the ANC, there was a process in which organs of civil society – trade unions, churches and NGOs – took part, not only enabling the process to move forward but also raising suggestions and demands regarding the conduct of the negotiations themselves.

The Palestine-Israel peace process, however, followed completely different lines. Even if there was a formal declaration of a ceasefire between the parties, there was no amnesty for Palestinian political prisoners. The building of settlements in the territories occupied by Israel continued undisturbed, and the Israeli government kept up a policy of summary execution of Palestinian activists, while refusing to allow the development of an independent and sovereign Palestinian State, which might have served as a means for moving from a ceasefire process to a peace process. At the same time, even if Israeli civil society brought pressure to bear on the Israeli institutions to initiate a peace process, it demobilized itself during the very process, leaving political society and its contradictory interests to monopolize the process.

In April 2000, after seven years of peace process, 135 Palestinian intellectuals published an open letter to the Israeli and Jewish public in the newspaper *Ha'aretz*. In it, the signatories said that the current events, instead of sowing seeds of peace, were preparing the next war: 'The great majority of Palestinians, including us, are convinced that the time has come for an agreement of understanding and for peace between ourselves and the Israelis. An agreement that would allow us to lead a normal, peaceful life in this land, free from the injustices, suffering and plunder that our people have suffered at the hands of the Israelis. This same Palestinian majority believes that peace will be based on two principles: justice and our joint needs for life in the future.' This open letter went on to say that the reality of the situation was very different, 'since one of the parties to the conflict, knowing it has the balance of power in its favour, is prepared to denigrate the other and force it to accept whatever proposal. So the hoped-for historic agreement is becoming an agreement between the Israelis and themselves and not with the Palestinians.'

This open letter marked the last time the voice of reason was heard in the framework of the Palestine-Israel conflict. A few months later, during the Camp David summit, Ehud Barak, the Israeli Prime Minister, tried to force the Palestinian President, Yasser Arafat, to capitulate and abandon the basic principles of the Palestine struggle for national liberation. Barak, assuming that the weakness of the Palestinian President's position would leave him no alternative, proposed to Arafat, in the form of a dictated ultimatum, the creation of a formally independent but not sovereign Palestinian state, in return for Palestinian renunciation of the right to return (to the territories from which they had been expelled, most in 1948) and a declaration by the Palestinians that the conflict and had come to an end and that there would be no further Palestinian claims.

Not only did Arafat not accept – and could not have accepted – the Israeli ultimatum, but Palestinians saw the attitude of the Israeli Prime Minister as reflecting their daily experience during the previous seven years: Israel's policy of total control, a complete lack of respect for Palestinians as people or for their aspirations or for their property, and finally the lack of readiness to make even minimal concessions with regard to the hopes and dreams of the Palestinian people. In this way, Barak gave voice to force, and the Palestinian uprising became only a question of time. And that marked the end of the Israeli–Palestinian peace process.

The 'Declaration of Principles' (DoP) signed in Washington on 13 September 1993 had regulated the political relationship between Israel and the Palestinians for seven years. These agreements, also known as 'the Oslo accords', as they had been negotiated in the Norwegian capital, had the aim of creating conditions that would lead to a negotiated peace between Palestinians and Israelis in a gradual process that would take five years.

These agreements had been intelligently designed so that each step forward would establish credibility between the parties and at the same time would accomplish concrete moves on the ground that could make the peace process sustainable. So, for example, the DoP established the Palestinian National Authority as the embryo of an independent Palestinian government, while at the same time creating regional and international conditions for reconstructing the Palestinian economy and political conditions for establishing organs of Palestinian civil society, which Israel had prohibited until then.

Problematically, Israel had not accepted the intervention of a third party, which would monitor the process and the application of the agreements, so the DoP was based on the good faith of both parties. The lack of monitors and the fact that no mechanisms had been put in place that might allow the political process to make progress in times of crisis – when good faith had vanished – left the process at the mercy of the interpretation either party placed on the agreements signed and of the balance of power between them. In other words, the peace process was left at the mercy of the interpretation placed on it by Israel, since Israel held the military and economic power in the region.

II. Zionism: Israel's official ideology

The state of Israel is the political expression of the movement of Zionist settlement. Zionism as an ideology and as a movement began in Central Europe in the late nineteenth century. The Zionist movement had two main objectives: the settlement of Palestine and the creation of a Jewish state.

Zionism was a Jewish expression of the nationalist revival in Eastern Europe during the 1840s. Just as happened with other nationalist revivals, the first expressions of Jewish nationalism were the rebirth of the language – Hebrew – and the adoption of romantic attitudes that saw emigration to Palestine – the historical cradle of the people – and settlement on its land as the only redemption that would allow a return to a heroic past, contrasted to a degraded present. In the mythic past postulated by nationalist romanticism, the Jews were a people of combative producers, in contradistinction to the present, in which they had become a people of victims and small traders.

Zionism interpreted the oppression of Jews in Eastern Europe not as a consequence of the social and political conditions of the region but as an essential characteristic of the ethical and moral corruption of the people during their long exile. In the Diaspora, Jews had adopted a parasitic way of life, living off the Gentiles, and so Gentile hatred of them was natural, and in this way Jews had become victims. Therefore the nationalist revolution had to involve not only the creation of Jewish sovereignty in Palestine, the mythical land, but also the regeneration of the Jewish character.

The settlement of Palestine was carried out through the establishment of two different sorts of cities and agricultural colonies. Some were to produce products for the international market, and in these the settlers employed local (Arab/Palestinian) labour, thereby creating a society similar to that of South African *apartheid*. Others adopted a practice that harked back to the nationalist revolutionary vision: for these, the purpose of emigration to Palestine was the regeneration of Jews, excluding the native Arab-Palestinian population. In its revolutionary form, Zionist nationalism came to invoke ethnic purity as the central element in the redemption of the land and people of Israel.

The British crown, under which Palestine was governed from the end of the First World War, allowed both the material advent of Jewish settlement and its practices, which from the very start brought about the exploitation of Palestinians, the impoverishment of their communities, and the eventual ethnic cleansing of the settled regions. But it was with the creation of the state of Israel in 1948 that ethnic cleansing reached its zenith with the deportation of 90 per cent of the Palestinian population from the new state territories. The remaining 10 per cent of the Palestinian population in Israel had to integrate as best they could under conditions of continual segregation and repression.

Zionist ideology, which postulates an exclusively Jewish state and continued settlement, is still the official ideology and policy of Israel. In this way Israel settled the territories conquered and depopulated during the 1948 war, and then the West Bank and Gaza Strip after the 1967 conquests. Israel has never mitigated its settlement ambitions, not even during the peace process. For example, in the period from 1993 to 2000 the number of settlers in the West Bank (excluding East Jerusalem) and Gaza Strip doubled, from 100,000 in 1993 to 200,000 in 2000.

III. The Palestinian case and the application of international regulations

The objectives of the Palestinian national struggle do not go beyond the framework of UN resolutions: 1. the creation of an independent and sovereign State of Palestine (General Assembly Resolution 181); 2. the right of Palestinian refugees to return (General Assembly Resolution 194); the withdrawal of Israeli troops from the West Bank and Gaza Strip (Security Council Resolutions 242 and 338). Subsequently, the organizations that make up the PLO have demanded that Israel comply with its obligations under the Fourth Geneva Convention as long as Israeli occupation continues.

Compliance with and application of international law and the UN resolutions would, however, damage the Zionist settlement programme. In the same way, if the resolutions of the international community were imposed, Israel's character as an exclusive ethnic state would be endangered. This means that the state of Israel is in a position of opposition to the framework of reference for resolving the Palestine-Israel conflict – respect for and compliance with the resolutions of the international community. This in turn means that the state of Israel finds itself in conflict not only with the Palestinian people but also with the international community.

In 1993 Israel agreed to enter into negotiations over the future of the territories occupied in 1967 only on condition that these would be bilateral negotiations and with no reference to international regulations. In this way the rights of the Palestinian people were set aside, since it meant that it was the balance of power, not international resolutions, that dictated the agreements reached between the two sides.

In their April 2000 declaration the Palestinian intellectuals said that 'history has shown that only those agreements based on mutual recognition, justice, and equality have been sustainable, while those agreements that were based on force and denigration led to further wars and disasters'. The disaster began on 29 September 2000.

IV. The challenge to civil society

On Friday 29 September 2000 five Muslim faithful were shot by Israeli police on the *Haram al Sharif* terrace while they were protesting about Ariel Sharon's visit to the site the previous day. The *Haram al Sharif*, the terrace of mosques in Jerusalem, known by Christians and Jews as the 'Temple Mount', is the third sacred site of Islam. According to the tradition of the monotheist religions, this is the site on which the temple of Solomon stood, and in the Muslim tradition it is also the place from which Muhammad ascended into heaven. *Haram al Sharif* for some, Temple Mount for others, the place has become an explosive national and religious symbol fought over by both sides. The police shots were interpreted as a profanation of a sacred place. On the Saturday at midday, television stations across the world transmitted pictures of Muhamad-a-Dura, a Palestinian boy, dying in his father's arms in Gaza during a demonstration against the profanation of the *haram*. The demonstrations extended to the Palestinian population living in Israel. The policy of the Israeli army – which was prepared for a Palestinian uprising at any time – was to repress any manifestation of popular dissatisfaction immediately and with firearms, and so the numbers of dead built up both within the Occupied Territories and among the Palestinian community living in Israel.

Organs of civil society in Israel, which during seven years of peace process had generally been supportive of the institutional policy of the Israeli government, had de-politicized and demobilized themselves and did not react to the killing and repression. On the contrary, they supported government policy, seeing the Palestine National Authority as responsible for the new wave of violence. In this way the fragile threads of dialogue that still existed were snapped.

Only small groups representing minorities had the courage to challenge government policy. These were conscientious objectors, the women's movement, and a new group formed to support the principles of the uprising – *Ta'ayush*, Arabic for 'coexistence'. This group of Israeli activists and Palestinian Israeli citizens declared that if the struggle for peace was not at the same time a joint Israeli–Palestinian struggle for equality and justice, it would not be a true struggle for peace but would revert to the institutional postulates of confrontation between the two peoples. The vision of a joint Arab–Jewish struggle was also put forward by the women's movement, in which Jewish women and Palestinian women living in Israel cooperate, and which carries out joint projects with feminist organizations in the Occupied Territories. Finally, the group of conscientious objectors questioned the militarist concept of the state and the legitimacy of the executive branch using the army as a force for repression.

These three movements formed the nucleus of a new political expression within Israeli society, which not only put forward a peace process but also challenged Israel's overall policy of occupation and settlement. While during the Oslo process there had been a sector of Israeli society on the side of peace, the *intifada* produced and nurtured a sector opposed to occupation that, unlike the earlier movement, challenged the official state ideology, Zionism.

V. Towards peace and reconciliation

The peace process that opened in 1993 did not have the aim of restricting the settlement programme that was the outcome of the nature of the state of Israel and its official ideology, and so conditions for enforcing a ceasefire could never be established: political prisoners were not set free, and the settlement of the West Bank and Gaza Strip continued unabated. Furthermore, while during the process first the PLO and then the Palestine National Authority recognized the legitimacy of the state of Israel, the latter never accepted the legitimacy of Palestinian claims during a bilateral process that highlighted the differences in economic, military and political strength between the two sides.

For a first step towards a peace process between Palestinians and Israelis to be possible, a ceasefire between the two sides has to be imposed, and this be cannot be done without the intervention of the international community to impose the rules of international law on the parties to the conflict, thus breaking the bilateral condition imposed by Israel. This would be but a first step forward, but it would open a space for dialogue between Israelis and Palestinians. A ceasefire would make room for dissident movements within Israeli society to put forward alternatives to the official state ideology, and this would be a great step forward as well as a process of reconciliation between Palestinians and Israelis. But as long as the international community does not intervene and restrain Israel's settlement policies, space for dialogue and negotiation between both communities will remain closed off, giving rise to fresh violence and death.

Translated by Paul Burns

Epilogue: 'Turning back History'

> '*Only in a spirit of utopia and with hope can one have the faith and courage to attempt, together with all the poor and downtrodden of the world, to turn back history, to subvert it and launch it in a different direction.*'[1]

With these words of Ignacio Ellacuría, spoken on 6 November 1989, ten days before his assassination, I should like, by way of epilogue, to reflect briefly on the theme 'A different world is possible', on *what* this 'different' world would be, on the spirit *in which* we have to work for it, and on the 'international' that can make it possible.

I. A different world is possible: the civilization of poverty

(a) In the last ten years of his life, seeing the direction in which the world was moving, particularly in the West, Ellacuría was absolutely convinced that a 'different' world was needed to save us from descending into inhumanity. This view is shared by many, but less so the solution he envisaged. He defined this as *the civilization of poverty*,[2] and stuck to it to the end of his life, pretty much alone, except – as far as I know – for Pedro Casaldáliga: 'The "civilization of love" should be complemented by what the Jesuit, Spanish, Basque, Salvadoran theologian Ellacuría has called "the civilization of poverty".'[3]

It is easy – at least in wish – to sign up to this 'different' world and to the 'civilization of love'. But the civilization of poverty requires the dismantling of the present world, and so a radical difference. And it involves the overthrow of the basic dogma of the West: that the world turns around the hinge of wealth. Ellacuría knew his proposal was shocking, but he stood by it. Let me explain briefly what he meant.

(b) Above all, the civilization of poverty is defined as such *in contradistinction* to the civilization of wealth and not, obviously, because it sets forth universal impoverishment as an ideal of life. What Ellacuría means is that in a world sinfully structured by the capital-wealth dynamic we need to encourage a different dynamic with a saving purpose. In this way, the civilization of poverty 'rejects the accumulation of capital as the energizer of history and the possession-enjoyment of wealth as principle of humanization. It makes the universal satisfying of basic needs the principle of development, and the growth of shared solidarity the foundation of humanization.'4

These statements are not mere theory. For a start, a civilization of universal wealth is impossible, since the world's resources will not allow everyone to live like this, like Europeans or North Americans. And this also makes it immoral, since, even without citing Jesus' parable of the rich man and the poor man, a solution than cannot be universalized cannot be a human solution, as Kant states in his *Critique of Practical Reason*. Furthermore, the civilization of wealth not only has not produced life for all: neither has it produced – with the exception of a few enclaves – 'civilization' in the sense of joy of human sharing, the spirit of courtesy – all of which means nothing to those who Darwinistically look only at the *species*, but it does concern those who want a human *family*.

The civilization of wealth has failed, but what does the civilization of poverty look like? Ellacuría described it – somewhat tortuously – in these words: 'This poverty is what truly gives the human spirit space, releasing it from the urge to have more than the next man, from the concupiscent urge to possess all sorts of non-necessities, when the greater part of humanity lacks necessities. This will make possible a flowering of the spirit, of the immense spiritual and human riches of the poor and the nations of the Third World, today sunk in wretchedness and under the domination of cultural models that may be developed in some aspects but are still not fully human.'5

Ellacuría sees it as obvious that a civilization worthy of the name must satisfy basic needs, and that only through this can there be 'a different world'. He devoted himself body and soul to this task, and that is why he was killed. But he increasingly felt the need for a civilization that could satisfy the needs of the spirit, meaning that its structures would make it possible for human beings to live 'civilizedly', 'humanly', 'with spirit', all of which he regarded as virtually impossible in a civilization of wealth. This offers the human spirit the ideal of 'the individual', of 'success', of 'standard of living'. And even though this ideal is promoted and sold as the fruits of democracy, it does not 'humanize', or 'civilize', or generate a 'different' world whose 'difference' will be good and whose 'depth' will reach down into the root of what it is to be human, to be persons, to be peoples.

The civilization of wealth 'civilizes' even less when it is seen not as the inheritance but as the 'manifest destiny' of the West, which justifies it in imposing its will and its interests on the rest of the world, blessing it as imperial ruler, as secular missionary of the wealth-divinity, and as generous benefactor.

II. Spirit: 'having faith and courage'

The civilization of poverty is the replacement for the civilization of wealth, and Ellacuría sees it as this 'different' world that we claim to be possible. What needs working out is *how* a world structured as a civilization of poverty is 'possible'. If we are to build it, clearly we need both theory and praxis, and this is why Ellacuría ended the sentence I have used to head this piece: 'There is another equally basic step, which is to create economic, political and cultural models that will make a civilization of work a possible substitute for a civilization of capital.'[6] But this step is preceded by another: 'Only in a spirit of utopia and with hope can one have the faith and courage [the need for spirit] to attempt [i.e., praxis]' to make another world. Making this different world possible demands 'praxis with spirit'. And this spirit is the hinge on which praxis and theory have to hang.

There are always hinges in history, but they often make what depends on them bad. Power and pleasure, individualism and pride in persons; imperialism, domination, overriding, crushing in institutions: both are frequent and normal 'hinges'. They keep the world as we know it turning.

There are also good hinges, many of which stem from differing traditions, above all religious. Religions have their dangers, but I want to look now at their potential for making the world hang well from a good hinge. I shall do so from within one tradition, that of following Jesus, on which other religious and secular traditions can converge and which they can also enrich.

Central to this tradition is *honesty with reality and living in reality*, meaning overcoming deceit and lies, as well as docetism, living in unreality, in little islands of abundance, which are exceptional and anecdotal on the planet (the permanent problem of the First World). Central too are the absoluteness of *compassion* for the suffering of others – 'those who suffer', Metz's phrase; *prophecy against injustice* that gives death, and the imperious *need for* justice in the face of the oppression against which we must struggle, not just mitigate ('justice' and 'injustice' being, of course, words that have been banished from our language); *care* for nature and the whole of creation, within which we all form a living whole; *mysticism* in the face of the ultimate *mystery* of existence, but an open-eyed mysticism; *stepping outside of oneself,* as in the prayer of St Francis of Assisi; *freedom,* so that nothing can stand in the way of doing good; *shouldering the burden of history* every day and to its end in *martyrdom*; the *memory* of martyrs and victims as the root on whose sap we live, which cannot be replaced by any other sap; the *joy* of knowing that we are all brothers and sisters, which can go hand in hand with suffering but can never be struck down with sadness; *naming* the ultimate affectionately as Father or Mother but without taking away the ineffability and mystery of God.

And I should like to add what is most often forgotten – a real scandal – and has been recovered through the biblical-Jesus tradition: *naming* the millions of this world's victims. They have been left without a name, which means that they have been deprived of their very existence. Suffice it to recall Africa, the non-existent continent, and many other millions of victims. Bringing them back to life, giving them dignified names, as Archbishop Romero and Ignacio Ellacuría did by calling them 'crucified people' and 'suffering servant of Yahweh', is an absolutely urgent human and theologal task. I believe it shares in the same audacity as naming God, and it may even be the historical mediation of naming mystery. It involves fomenting their memory in history, but it goes beyond that. It is bringing mystery to mind throughout history and having the hope that the future will also be mystery, a blessed promise of welcome. And in the end, this tradition also shows the greatest love: laying down one's life for others.

These expressions of spirit are needed as the hinge on which a 'different' world, and specifically a civilization of poverty, can swing open. The fact that they have been exemplified in Jesus of Nazareth does not imply falling into any sort of dogmatism; it simply helps to formulate a centre of gravity on which other traditions can converge. In fact compassion, care, prophecy, self-denying love and the like have many mothers. The important thing is that they should cohere around one axis on which a human world can turn.

It is also important for this coherence to be the product of not only a dia-*logue* but also a dia-*praxis*. And ultimately for all those, men and women, who desire a genuinely 'different' world to cohere around, to feel the attraction of – to use a metaphor with powerful physical overtones – a centre of gravity that fuses them through the spirit I have described – or through the spirit that looks best. The important thing is that this centre of gravity is not just a matter of knowledge and power but is also a matter of spirit.

It is not easy to know what part the early Christians played in the downfall of the Roman Empire. What is certain is that the new values by which they lived and died, exemplified in the simplicity of monasteries and communities, pointed to 'another' world, to a different future and a new way of living. This is how they took on the 'old' world of the empire and the strength of its legions, as Felix Wilfred clearly shows in his article.

I am not ingenuous, but without spirit there will be no 'different' world. And if I have dwelt on this, it is because the present world has, pre-eminently, a spirit deficit. Let us ask in all seriousness: Are there many people in the present, Western, democratic world who want to take up the cross of Africans, Asians, and Latin Americans to make a 'different' world possible? Are they prepared to end their days on a cross, like so many martyrs of our time, so that compassion, truth, and justice may reign over this world? Leonardo Boff has said, 'When they judge our age, future generations will stigmatize us as barbarians, inhuman and pitiless on account of our vast insensitivity to the sufferings of our own brothers and sisters.'[7] Are words such as these sufficient spur and goad to build 'another' world and to change the hinge from which the present one hangs?

III. Who: 'With all the poor and oppressed of the world'

The building of a different world, of a civilization of poverty, obviously has to spread among many people. It is both good and necessary to seek alliances among different groups and to build up strength to eradicate the sinfulness of the present world. But the decisive element, the *sine qua non*, is that the spirit I have described should be above all a spirit rising up from the real poor. We can again resort to the different traditions and make them converge on the ideal we have set forward, but they are not all equal. The tradition of democracy, for example, so important in other aspects, does not put the poor at the centre, even though Marxism, in its way, tried to. The Asian and African religious traditions have been foremost in doing this, to which they add that poverty is not just a negative value.

The biblical-Jesus tradition truly is clear on the subject of the poor and the salvation they bring.[8] Without being either ingenuous or absurd, it recognizes that the humanizing 'spirit' resides more in the poor than elsewhere. *Salvation* supposes promise and, correlatively, hope, specifically hope in brotherhood, in solidarity, in the shared table. But what is special to this tradition is that the dynamic of salvation comes not from the great and powerful but from what is small and weak: a sterile old woman, the tiny people of Israel, a Jew from the edge of empire.

In order to change the world we evidently need politicians, economists, engineers, philosophers, but the centre of the dynamic of salvation lies in what is weak and little. They are its bearers as well as its beneficiaries. Utopia responds to their hopes, not to those of the powerful. Their littleness expresses the gratuitousness of salvation, not the *hybris* that leads to destruction rather than construction. This tradition of littleness that saves runs through scripture, but this is not all. In the Old Testament there appears the mysterious figure of the suffering servant of Yahweh, who is not only 'poor' and 'little' but 'victim'. And we are told that this servant has been chosen by God to take away the sin of the world and to bring salvation. To the scandal of littleness there is now added the folly of victimhood. As Ellacuría said, 'Only through a difficult act of faith is the singer of the servant able to discover what appears as the complete opposite in the eyes of history.'[9]

A great spirit of subtlety, as Pascal says, is needed for this faith, but it does occur – not just anywhere, but in the midst of the crucified peoples. I have often given examples of it. From Asia, Fr Aloysius Pieris wrote that the poor are chosen for a mission, not because they are holy but because they are powerless, rejected: 'They are summoned to be mediators of the salvation of the rich, and the weak are called to liberate the strong.'[10] From Africa, E. Mveng wrote, 'The church of Africa . . . through its poverty and its humility should remind all its sister churches of the essence of the beatitudes and proclaim the good news of liberation to those who have succumbed to the temptation of power, wealth and domination.'[11]

One final point: in the old days there were 'masters of suspicion', of religion and God above all. Today we no longer see the audacity to be suspicious of not just the great idols – of which there is some evidence – but of the present-day world itself, and – more subtly – of democracy, of prosperity, of progress; it is as though they were untouchable, despite Moltmann's insistence on speaking of 'progress and precipice'. The poor of this world can – by virtue of their very situation – be the great masters of suspicion, and this is no small service they can provide in making sure that there is no deceit in the quest for a 'different' world.

IV. The setting: 'in a spirit of utopia and with hope'

It was important earlier to determine the setting from which to see the situation and to read the texts, since the right setting made both situation and texts reveal more of themselves. Now this hermeneutical approach is not so common, but it is still essential in dealing with this 'different' possible world: the place from where we decide what it is and how it is to be built.

I have already mentioned traditions that facilitate the task, but here I should like to indicate the setting in which what looks most like madness and capriciousness in these remarks (the civilization of poverty) is in fact the most rational and necessary (the building of universal brother- and sister-hood). Ellacuría saw the problem with total clarity and stressed that this setting is not any setting but that in which – by its nature rather than through the will of individuals – utopia and prophecy converge.[12]

The decisive factor in being able to think – and having to do so – of a 'different' world as a civilization of poverty is seeing utopia and prophecy in conjunction and intrinsic mutual reference to one another. Prophecy should not be seen, in isolation, as *denunciation* of a present evil, nor should utopia be seen, in isolation, as *proclamation* of a future good. They should be seen dialectically, each referring to the other, as expressions of the dynamic of the same process. In simple terms, utopia and prophecy do not stem from a world that is *tabula rasa*, that can lead to one thing or another, that can be selected at people's discretion. Reality itself, prior to human will or caprice, is what gives voice, in the form of a clamour of protest and denial and in the form of groans in birth pangs promising life and bringing life into being.

In this way, when we take both things, utopia and prophecy, as one, we are then in harmony with reality. The conjoining of both things does not just become a mental construct but is required by reality itself. This is why it is important to find the social and historical settings in which prophecy and utopia really converge and lead us to a 'different' and definitively 'human' world.

Now not all settings are equal: 'There are certain places more propitious to the rise of prophetic utopians and of utopian prophets.'[13] Specifically to the present subject, the setting in which to believe that 'a different world is possible', let alone to formulate it as a 'civilization of poverty', is not the world of abundance, of exaltation of the individual, of success and standard of living. Still less is it the world of the overbearing 'reality is us'. The setting in which utopia and prophecy of necessity converge is the Third World, in which the scale of injustice and death is intolerable, and where justice and life are as necessary as water in the desert.

From here, prophecy does not become mere subjective protest, nor does utopia become esoteric and capricious. Rather, they both become a protest against death and ignominy on the basis of hope for life and dignity. From this setting there can be little doubt of the direction this 'different' world for which we hope should take. The route is that of the 'civilization of poverty'. In simple terms, Boston, Paris and Madrid have no reason to be places clamouring for a civilization of poverty, whereas Kigali, Calcutta and Haiti have.

I should like to end with another quotation from Ellacuría, also dating from 1989 – shocking and ironic, but also lucid and questioning, even rhetorical:

All that martyr blood spilt in El Salvador and throughout Latin America, far from moving us to discouragement and despair, infuses a new spirit of struggle and new hope in our people. In this sense, if we are not a 'new world' or a 'new continent', we clearly and verifiably – and not just by outsiders – are a continent of hope, which is a strikingly interesting symptom of a future creation compared to other continents that have no hope but have only fear.[14]

I do not know what Ellacuría would say today, fifteen years later, but I cite these words because they are the final ones of his article, and this brings to my mind the ending of Mark (16.8) before it was retouched and its tone of terror moderated: 'So they went out and fled from the tomb, for terror and amazement had seized them; and they said nothing to anyone, for they were afraid.'

Both texts end in a nosedive, but neither Mark nor Ellacuría can be accused of being masochists. They were proclaiming good news: the gospel of Jesus, in Mark's case; the civilization of poverty, in Ellacuría's, and they retained their hope. They did not belittle events but put their whole lives into their purpose. Perhaps this mention of them may give light and heart to all those who work to make 'a different world possible'.

Translated by Paul Burns

Notes

1. 'El desafío de las mayorías populares', *ECA* 493–4, 1989, p.1078.
2. 'The Kingdom of God and Unemployment in the Third World', *Concilium* 1982/10, pp.91–6; 'Misión actual de la Compañía de Jesús', written in 1983 and published posthumously in *RLT* 29, 1993, pp.115–26; 'Utopia and Prophecy in Latin America', reprinted in I. Ellacuría and J. Sobrino (eds), *Mysterium Liberationis. Fundamental Concepts of Liberation Theology*, Maryknoll, NY 1993, pp. 289–328.
3. 'A los quinientos años: "decolonizar" y "desevengelizar"', *RLT* 16, 1989, p. 118. Casaldáliga spoke later of the civilization of 'poverty in solidarity'.

4. 'Utopia and Prophecy' (n.2), p. 315.

5. 'Misión actual' (n.2), pp.119f.

6. 'El desafio'(n.1), p.1078.

7. L. Boff, *La oración de San Francisco*, Santander 1999, p. 98.

8. I have developed these ideas at greater length in 'La opción por los pobres: dar y recibir. "Humanizar la humanided"', *RLT* 18, 1989, pp. 283–307.

9. I. Ellacuría, 'El pueblo crucificado. Ensayo de soterología histórica', *RLT* 18, p. 326.

10. A. Pieris, 'Cristo más allá del dogma. Hacer cristología en el contexto de las religiones de los pobres (1)', *RLT* 52, 2001, p.16.

11. Engelbert Mveng, 'Iglesia y solidaridad con los pobres de Africa: empobrecimiento antropológico' in *Identidad africana y cristiana*, Estella, 1999, pp. 273ff. Mveng, the first Jesuit from Cameroon, was assassinated in 1995.

12. See his article 'Utopía y profetismo desde América Latina. Un ensayo concreto de soterología histórica', *RLT* 17, 1989, pp. 141–84.

13. Ibid., p. 141.

14. 'Quinto centenario de América Latina. ¿Descubrimiento o encubrimiento?', *RLT* 21, 1990, pp.280ff.

Contributors

LUIZ CARLOS SUSIN teaches systematic theology at the Pontifical Catholic University of Porto Alegre in Brazil and at the Franciscan College of Theology and Spirituality in the same city. He is a member of the Order of Capuchin Friars and an adviser to the Brazilian Conference of Religious. His doctoral thesis was on the thought of Emanuel Levinas, and his concerns are the frontiers between theology, philosophy and anthropology. He has recently been investigating the relationship between theology and ecology, and his latest book is a *Criação de Deus* (God's Creation, 2003).

Address: Rua Juarez Távora 171, 91520-100 Porto Alegre RS, Brazil

WIM DIERCKXSENS was born in Holland in 1946 and holds a doctorate in social sciences from the University of Nijmegen, with a postgraduate degree in demography from the Sorbonne. He has worked for the United Nations, researched and lectured at the University of Brabant, and been a government adviser in the Netherlands. He has worked in Central America since 1971 and is at present a researcher for the DEI in San José, Costa Rica, coordinating the research of the World Alternatives Forum and directing its Latin American Secretariat. He has published several books in various languages on alternatives to neo-liberalism, including *The Limits of Capitalism* (2000), *Del neoliberalismo al postcapitalismo* (2000), *El ocaso del capitalismo y la utopía reencontrada* (2003) and *Guerra global, resistencia mundial y alternativas* (2004).

Address: Apartado 171, CP2070, Costa Rica

CÂNDIDO GRZYBOWSKI has been the Director of the Brazilian Institute of Social and Economic Analyses (IBASE) since 1990. A philosopher and sociologist, he holds a doctorate from the University of Paris I (Panthéon-Sorbonne) and did post-doctoral studies at University College London. A former Professor of Sociology of Development at the Fundação Getúlio Vargas in Rio de Janeiro (1989–1991), he was a member of the organizing committee of the World Social Forum (2001–2003) and serves in its international secretariat. He has published books and articles on social movements, civil society, democracy and globalization. IBASE has been at the centre of many public campaigns in Brazil, and the main areas of its work today are: food security, solidarity economy, democratic alternatives to globalization, participation in civil society, public policies, social watch, democratization of big cities, the ethics and social responsibility of organizations.

Address: Av. Rio Branco, 124, 8° andar, Rio de Janeiro – RJ – Brasil, Cep 20148-900
Email: candido@ibase.br

JOSÉ MARÍA CASTILLO SÁNCHEZ, SJ, was born in the province of Granada in Spain in 1929. He has a doctorate in dogmatic theology from the Gregorianum and has held the chair of theology at Granada University, from which he was dismissed after Vatican pressure on the Jesuit General in 1988. From 1990 to 2002 he was visiting professor at the University of Central America in El Salvador. Since 1977 he has concerned himself with 'popular theology', has been ideologically linked with liberation theology, and has been an active collaborator in grassroots Christian movements. He was a co-founder of the John XXIII Association of Theologians and remains on its governing body. His many published works include *Oración y existencia cristiana* (1968), *La alternativa cristiana* (1975), *El seguimiento de Jesús* (1983), *Los pobres y la teología* (1998), and *El Reino de Dios. Por la vida y la dignidad de los seres humanos* (2000). He has also collaborated in various encyclopaedic works and contributed more than 150 articles to learned and popular journals.

Address: Paseo de Cartuja, 35 – 3°, 18012 Granada, Spain

SALLIE MCFAGUE is Distinguished Theologian in Residence at the Vancouver School of Theology in British Columbia, Canada. She writes extensively on theology and ecology, with her most recent book being *Life Abundant: Rethinking Theology and Economy for a Planet in Peril* , Minneapolis 2000.

Address: Vancouver School of Theology, 6050 Iona Drive, Vancouver, BC Canada V6T 1L4

MUSIMBI KANYORO is the General Secretary of the World Young Women's Christian Association (World YWCA), the largest and oldest women's ecumenical movement serving 25 million women and girls in 122 countries. She has more than two decades of international experience in working with non-governmental organizations (NGOs), churches and ecumenical institutions on a wide variety of issues, including social and economic development, organizational development, human resources and leadership development. She has provided various aspects of leadership in the preparation and implementation of major UN conferences including the Fourth World Conference on Women held in Beijing in 1995. She serves on three major committees of the UNAIDS. During her leadership, the World YWCA has made HIV/AIDS a priority programme. Musimbi Kanyoro also serves on a number of ecumenical and NGO boards and is the current president of the World Association for Christian Communication (WACC) with headquarters in London.

Address: World Young Women's Christian Association, 16, Ancienne Route, 1218 Grand Saconnex, Switzerland
E-mail: musimbi.kanyoro@worldywca.org

PERRY SCHMIDT-LEUKEL is Professor of Systematic Theology and Religious Studies and Director of the Centre for Inter-Faith Studies at the University of Glasgow. He has published widely in the field of fundamental theology, theology of religions, and Christian-Buddhist dialogue. Most recently he edited *War and Peace in World Religions*, London 2004. He has just completed a major work on religious pluralism which will be published in 2005.

Address: University of Glasgow, Department of Theology and Religious Studies, 4 The Square, Glasgow G12 8QQ

CLAUDE GEFFRÉ, a Dominican theologian, taught at the Dominican faculties of Le Saulchoir, of which he was Rector from 1965 to 1968. He was then appointed professor in the theological faculty of the Institut catholique de Paris, where for a long time he taught fundamental theology, hermeneutical theology and the theology of religions. Since 1996 he has been an honorary professor at the Institut catholique, and was appointed Director of the École biblique in Jerusalem. He is still editor of the series Cogitatio Fidei. Recent works include: *Profession théologien. Quelle pensée chrétienne pour le XXIème siècle?*, Paris 1999; *Croire et interpréter. Le tournant herméneutique de la théologie*, Paris 2001.

Address : 143, Bd Raspail, 75006 Paris
E-mail : clgeffre@free.fr

ÉLOI MESSI METOGO was born in Cameroon in 1952; he is a Dominican. He gained a licenciate and a doctorate in theology at the Institut catholique de Paris and a doctorate in the history of religions at Paris IV-Sorbonne. He is currently professor of theology at the Catholic University of Central Africa in Yaoundé. His main publications are *Théologie africaine et ethno-philosophies. Problèmes de méthode en théologie africaine*, Paris 1985; *Dieu peut-il mourir en Afrique? Essai sur l'indifférence religieuse et l'incroyance en Afrique noire*, Paris and Yaoundé 1997.

Address: Université catholique d'Afrique Centrale, BP 11628, Yaoundé, Cameroon

FELIX WILFRED was born in Tamilnadu, India in 1948. He is professor in the School of Philosophy and Religious Thought, State University of Madras, India. He has taught, as visiting professor, in the universities of Nijmegen, Münster, Frankfurt am Main and Ateneo de Manila. He was also a member of the International Theological Commission of the Vatican. He has been president of the Indian Theological Association and Secretary of the Theological Commission of FABC. He is a member of the editorial board of *Concilium*. His researches and field studies today cut across many disciplines in humanities and social sciences. Among his publications in the field of theology are: *From the Dusty Soil. Reinterpretation of Christianity* (1995); *Beyond Settled Foundations. The Journey of Indian Theology* (1993); *Sunset in the East? Asian Challenges and Christian Involvement* (1991); *Leave the Temple* (1992).

Address: University of Madras, Dept of Christian Studies, Chepauk, Madras, India
E-mail: fwilfred@satyam.net.in

RUDOLF VON SINNER, born in 1967 in Basel, Switzerland, is Professor of Systematic Theology, Ecumenism and Interreligious Dialogue at the Escola Superior de Teologia in São Leopoldo, Brazil and a minister of the Evangelical Church of the Lutheran Confession in Brazil. He has published a variety of articles and chapters on ecumenical hermeneutics, contextual theology and ecumenical political ethics, as well as the book *Reden vom dreieinigen Gott in Brasilien und Indien. Grundzüge einer ökumenischen Hermeneutik im Dialog mit Leonardo Boff und Raimon Panikkar*, Tübingen 2003. He is currently working on a major research project on the Brazilian churches' contribution to *cidadania* (citizenship), supported by the Swiss National Science Foundation.

Address: Escola Superior de Teologia, Cx Postal 14, 93001-970 São Leopoldo-RS, Brazil
E-mail: r.vonsinner@est.com.br, www.est.com.br

JUNG MO SUNG was born in South Korea in 1957 and has lived in Brazil since 1966. He has a doctorate in religious studies and a post-doctorate in education. He teaches a post-graduate course in religious studies at both the Methodist and the Catholic universities in São Paulo, while doing research into the relationship between religion, economics and education. His published works include *Teologia e economia: repensando a teologia da libertação e utopias* (1994); *Desejo, mercado e religião* (1998); *Competência e sensibilidade solidária: educar para esperança* (with Hugo Assmann); and *Sujeito e sociedades complexas: para repensar os horizontes utópicos* (2002).

Address: R. Humberto I, 254, ap. 121-A, 04018-030 São Paulo – SP, Brazil
E-mail: jungmosung@uol.com.br

SERGIO YAHNI was born in Argentina and grew up on a kibbutz in Israel. He graduated in 1998 from the Hebrew University of Jerusalem, where he read history and philosophy. Since 1987 he has been an activist for peace and social justice in Israel, and he is also director of the Alternative Information Centre, a joint Israeli-Palestinian NGO with offices in Jerusalem and Bethlehem.

Address: The Alternative Information Centre, PO Box 31417, Jerusalem 91313, Israel.

JON SOBRINO was born in the Basque Country in 1938 and educated in Spain; Germany, where he gained a doctorate in theology; and the USA, from where, unique among liberation theologians, he holds a master's degree in mechanical engineering. He joined the Society of Jesus in 1956 and since 1957 has belonged to the Central American province and lived mainly in El Salvador. His many works translated into English include *Christology at the Crossroads* (1976); *The True Church and the Poor* (1984); *Jesus in Latin America* (1986); *Spirituality of Liberation* (1988); *Companions of Jesus. The Murder and Martyrdom of the Salvadorean Jesuits* (1990). With the late Ignacio Ellacuria, he was joint editor of *Mysterium Liberationis: Fundamental Concepts of Liberation Theology* (1993). The first volume of his two-volume christology, *Jesus the Liberator*, appeared in 1993, and the second, *Following Jesus,* in 2001.

Address: Universidad Centroamericana, Centro Monseñor Romero, Apartado (01) 168, San Salvador, El Salvador
E-mail: jsobrino@cmr.uca.edu.sv

The editors are most grateful to the following for their help in preparing this issue:

Nedjeljko A. Ančić
Erik Borgman
Richard G. Cote
Luis Alberto De Boni
Virgilio Elizondo
Michel de Goedt
Thomas H. Groome
Ottmar John
Hubert Lepargneur
Norbert Mette
John Riches
Andrés Torres de Queiruga

Concilium Subscription Information

February   2004/1: *Original Sin*

April   2004/2: *Rethinking Europe*

June   2004/3: *The Structural Betrayal of Trust*

October   2004/4: *Job's God*

December   2004/5: *A Different World is Possible*

New subscribers: to receive *Concilium* 2004 (five issues) anywhere in the world, please copy this form, complete it in block capitals and send it with your payment to the address below.

- -

Please enter my subscription for *Concilium* 2004

Individuals
____ £32.50 UK/Rest of World
____ $63.00 North America

Institutions
____ £48.50 UK/Rest of World
____ $93.50 North America

Please add £17.50/$33.50 for airmail delivery

Payment Details:
Payment must accompany all orders and can be made by cheque or credit card
I enclose a cheque for £/$ _____ Payable to SCM-Canterbury Press Ltd
Please charge my Visa/MasterCard (Delete as appropriate) for £/$ _____
Credit card number ....
Expiry date ....
Signature of cardholder ....
Name on card ....
Telephone .... E-mail ....

Send your order to *Concilium*, SCM-Canterbury Press Ltd
9–17 St Albans Place, London N1 ONX, UK
Tel +44 (0)20 7359 8033 Fax +44 (0)20 7359 0049
E-Mail: office@scm-canterburypress.co.uk

Customer service information:
All orders must be prepaid. Subscriptions are entered on an annual basis (i.e. January to December) No refunds on subscriptions will be made after the first issue of the Journal has been despatched. If you have any queries or require information about other payment methods, please contact our Customer services department.